Aw...Relax,
Archie!
Re-laxx!

To David and Ann

Hope you enjoy reading
the book —

Regards from next Door!   :-)

Hal (Harlan) Stone
AKA "Jughead"

11/10/02

Aw...Relax, Archie! Re-laxx!

When radio was "King"
I was once a "prince"
But ended up a "JUGHEAD"

by Hal Harlan Stone

Published by:

Bygone Days Press
Post Office Box 4418
Sedona, AZ 86340 U.S.A.

Printed by Fidlar Doubleday, Inc. Kalamazoo, MI.

Library of Congress Catalogue Card Number: 2002092154

ISBN: 0-9720170-0-3

TABLE OF CONTENTS

Acknowledgments

The reader will have to thank, (or blame) Charlie Summers for encouraging and inspiring me to write this "epic". I thank him profusely for his help, and patience, with my computer illiteracy.

For help with the content, I owe much to those who assisted in filling in my memory gaps. Primarily, my fellow actors, Bob Hastings, Rosemary Rice, Jane Webb, and my recently departed friend, Charles Harold Mullen. Then too, Elizabeth McLeod and Jay Hickerson, (both respected "experts" and researchers in the history of Old Time Radio) gave needed dates and times. In addition, one of the very active participants at Old Time Radio Conventions, B.J. Watkins, helped me connect names with faces. And I would be remiss if I didn't single out Bill Guggenheim, who in my opinion, is the #1 fan of the "Archie" program, having collected over 41 episodes of the show.

Being a borderline "computer illiterate", I have to thank the following people who guided me through some of the complicated software programs I had to learn. Mike White, who first set me up with the text program, and then, Jane Perini who solved problems when I kept messing up. As for the graphics software, the young whippersnapper Joan (Jeb) Richardson struggled, (successfully I hope) to teach an old dog new tricks. To Frank Benages of Fidlar/Doubleday for guiding me through the printing process.

To Janie Apfel, my good friend, for doing a heroic job on the proofreading and editing of the drafts.

And most definitely, my lovely wife Dorothy, for her support and encouragement whenever I'd get frustrated, her editorial expertise, suggestions, and invaluable internet research. Bless you.

Dedication

To the three women in my childhood who had such a profound and lasting effect on my life.

My Mother, Helen Frances McKinley Stone, who started me on my career path.

My "surrogate" Mom, the incredibly gifted and gracious actress Lillian Gish, who encouraged me as an actor, as well as an artist.

My mentor and muse, another wonderful actress, Elissa Landi, who encouraged a young child to pursue all forms of creative expression.

Without the early encouragement of these three very memorable individuals, I would not have had any noteworthy experiences, or recollections, to even attempt, (or possibly justify), writing a book about my early years.

— THE AUTHOR

Illustrations & Text

I have included so many photographs and illustrations in this book, that I will forego listing them all. As an artist and former TV director, I support the old adage, "One picture is worth a thousand words". However, a few I included might be worth only 500 words since the quality is less than perfect . Many of the photographs are reproduced from old prints. In early candids, the faces were quite small and didn't reproduce well when enlarged. Others, reproduced from newsprint and magazines, presented the old "dots per inch" problem. Although some are borderline quality, you can at least see what people looked like when I talk about them.

As mentioned previously, the "Archie" comic book characters were used with permission from Archie Comics Publications. All other "cartoon" drawings (used to illustrate a story or emphasize a point), were done by the author. (That's me.) I did not include the copyright symbol on any of those, but the rules apply. "They may not be reproduced in any fashion without the written permission from the author and/or publisher". Not that anyone would necessarily want to, but I have to say that just in case. ☺

I had fun assembling all of these graphics, and spent many hours trying to get the best quality possible from the original material. I hope they all help "tell" the story.

A quick note about the text. I used a lot of parenthesis for effect. In radio, the script writer would often put notes to the actor in parenthesis. Like (breathlessly), (agitated), (dejectedly), etc. That's how he wanted the lines delivered. I used parenthesis as an "aside" or an "under my breath comment" to color the story. They often denote great mock sarcasm, or hopefully, wry humor.

Preface

If you purchased this book, borrowed it, or simply picked it up someplace…(remember, shoplifting is a "no-no"), you have probably guessed (or know by looking at the cover) that I played Jughead on the "Adventures of Archie Andrews" radio program.

Although I played that role for many years, I had a varied career in show business. (This book also covers some of those other performing activities.) I certainly don't presume that my radio acting career was as notable as the achievements of many of my contemporaries, but my experiences were definitely unique, and fans of Old Time Radio (OTR) hunger for stories from those days.

The OTR fans of today are part of a vast "Hobby". A hobby wherein they collect recorded copies of many of the old radio programs. They either buy them from OTR dealers, trade among each other, and seek memorabilia, autographs and/or pictures of those who performed on the shows back in the '30s, '40s and '50's. In addition, they usually have in their libraries one or more books about this defunct, yet still popular entertainment industry that preceded TV. These OTR "Hobbyists" are, for the most part, responsible for my writing yet another book on the subject. They like hearing stories from a totally new source. Since not too many of us "Old Time Radio" actors are still around, the "well head" of information is drying up. It's my intent, with this book, not to let those fans down. I'll tell it like it was,(no candy coating), and let the chips fall where they may. But fair warning; I began performing at a very early age, so don't expect me to remember everything about those early years. But enough, I hope, to justify your spending good money if you purchased a copy. For which I thank you!

Forward

"Return with us now to those thrilling days of yesteryear. From out of the past come the thundering hoof beats of the great horse Silver. The Lone Ranger rides again. A fiery horse with the speed of light, a cloud of dust and a hearty Hi-Ho Silver, the Lone Ranger Rides Again".

"Hey Jughead, come over right away, it's a matter of life and death…Aw, Relax Archie, Reeelaxx."

What red blooded American growing up in the 1940's could ever forget those words? And others, like "Jack Armstrong, the All American Boy", "Wheaties, the breakfast of champions", "Mr. District Attorney", "David Harding-Counterspy", "Dick Tracy", "The Shadow", "Inner Sanctum", "Orson Wells", "Mr. Keen, Tracer of Lost Persons", The Hindenberg disaster, and most of all, FDR's address to the nation on December 8, 1941.

These were the days of radio. There was no TV, no Internet, no Zip Code, and operators still answered the phone. In the evening, the family huddled around the gigantic radio receiver in the living room. In the middle of the dial was a huge "cat's eye" peering out into the room to show that the set was tuned just right. We all had to keep quiet so Dad could listen to his favorite show.

In our home, the favorite show was "The Adventures of Archie Andrews". Of course, we had a selfish motive. My Dad, Louis, and my partner Richard's Dad, John, were the owners of Archie Comics. I can still hear my Dad going "Shush, Shush, I can't hear it", if my Mother or I made a sound.

X

As kids, Richard and I were celebrities. We "owned" Archie Comics. In those days, Archie sold one million copies of an issue.

One day, our fathers brought us to NBC to see "The Adventures of Archie Andrews" radio show. I remember walking into a studio and seeing a bunch of grown-ups standing around microphones with a bunch of papers in their hands. They were all reading from the scripts with funny voices. Off to the side, was a man making funny sound effects. An announcer would talk about Swift Premium Franks. It was just great. I can still see it today. I believe I even got autographs.

Today, Archie Comics are still America's leading teenage humor comics magazine. Our website, archiecomics.com receives more than eighteen million hits a month. Our comics are on sale at most supermarket checkouts and in most chain stores, book stores, convenience stores and drug store chains. I have no doubt that the success of the "Archie" program so many years ago helped us grow.

The autographs have long disappeared, and as we celebrate the diamond jubilee 60th anniversary of Archie Comics, it was a great surprise to hear from Harlan Stone, the voice of Jughead from my childhood days, and what an honor to be asked to write this introduction. Every time I think of the radio show, I hear Harlan's voice(as Jughead) telling Archie to "re-laxx!

So relax, and read on about this by gone era.

Michael Silberkleit
Chairman/Publisher
Archie Comic Publications, Inc.
Mamaroneck, New York, May, 2002

Overture

Orchestra plays "If They Asked Me, I Could Write a Book"

Many years ago, that was the title of a very popular love song; a perfect sentiment to start this "epic" tale. In keeping with the book's Show Biz theme, I'm using "Acts" and "Scenes" (and not normal chapters), in a playlet or script form. Don't ask me why! I was just getting creative in my old age. To set the stage for you, our "hero" in this story never planned on becoming an actor. That career just evolved, with definite stepping stones along the way.

Back in the days when Radio Broadcasting was our Country's "free" major entertainment medium, I had the good fortune to be steadily employed as an actor in that profession for about 15 years. I'm referring to the period of the 1940's through the mid 50's. This book then, is about what it was like for a young child growing up as a performer in radio broadcasting. Within these pages, I'll try to help the reader capture the flavor of those days, the atmosphere that we worked in, and what a typical radio actor usually encountered on a day to day basis. And I have to admit. It sure was fun!

The book title is derived from the standard opening of the "Archie Andrews" radio show.

SFX: (Phone ring. Receiver picked up)
JUGHEAD: Hello!
ARCHIE: Hello Jughead, this is Archie. Come over right
                   away. It's a matter of life and death!
JUGHEAD: Aw, relax, Archie. Ree-Laxx!

Act 1

Scene 1

(Music up and under) "You must have been a beautiful Baby"

(CUE NARRATION)

If you remember, in the preface of this book, I said that I didn't intend for this to be my autobiography.

Well, that's not totally accurate. I suppose I should at least tell you about my early childhood and how I ultimately became a Radio Actor... A sort of brief history about the path I took to get there. Or, more accurately... the path I was "led" down.

I was born in 1931. (They called us "Depression" babies back then.) My Mother was Scotch-Irish, my Father was the Iceman... I'm not kidding! (Of English and German ancestry).

Authors Note: Wow, this book is going to be harder to write than I thought. The above reference to my Father being the Iceman only has significance to those readers of my generation. Those under 65 will not get the joke and I probably shouldn't waste everyone's time trying to explain the "generation gap" stuff. Maybe I'll use footnotes if I encounter the problem again. But for you "kids" out there, I'll attempt an explanation, because it really does have a bearing on my story. (Please be patient, you "Old Timers").

Back in those post "Horse and Buggy" days, we didn't have refrigerators. Folks used an icebox to keep food from spoiling. And if one wanted to kid around and jokingly question someone's paternity , they would ask, *who was your Father, the Iceman?*" That reference was of course occasioned by the fact that the "Iceman" made daily deliveries of large blocks of ice to the housewives of the neighborhood. Why in heck the "Milkman" (who also made daily deliveries) wasn't blamed, I'll never know. But then again, the Milkman left his deliveries outside in the milkbox on the porch, while the Iceman, carrying the heavy block of ice on his shoulder, was led indoors to the kitchen icebox by the hapless housewives.

It probably also had something to do with the physique of the Iceman. To lift and carry those big chunks of ice (frequently up a few flights of stairs), was certain to develop big muscles, legs, and upper torso's for those in that occupation. You know, the "Bronze God" syndrome... which supposedly made the Iceman irresistible to females. (That explanation will have to suffice.)

2

The "put down" about the Iceman when questioning one's paternity was nothing more than a sarcastic expression of the times. Much like "*Aw, your Mother wears Combat Boots*" that we used during the 2nd World War. (I don't have to explain that one do I?)

Anyway, my Dad really was an Iceman. But as luck would have it, (of the "bad" sort), refrigeration came along, and his income slowly melted away. (I couldn't resist the pun, sorry!)

When my parents discovered that I could help out and also earn money for the family, my "Career" began at age 3. By then, I had a younger sister named Helen (also fathered by that same Iceman I'm happy to report), so my income was not only appreciated, but necessary. Fortunately, instead of my parents renting me out to some Sweat Shop industry, they discovered I could earn a buck or two the easy way. I became a "Child Model". And if you'll permit me to brag just a tiny bit, apparently I was very successful at it, eventually earning $10 bucks an hour. In the mid '30's, that was a small fortune. How much my parents got after agent's commission, travel expenses, etc. I'm not sure, but you better believe I was their pride and joy.

Now you have to understand... I don't remember too much about those early years. I was too damn young to grasp what was going on around me. But I do know that I wasn't unhappy or uncomfortable working as a child model. I liked the attention...... being fussed over...... and the "Bribes" .

Those came about in case I wasn't too thrilled at having to interrupt my playtime to go into NYC for a modeling job. (We lived out on Long Island, an hour's bus & subway ride away .)

And… I was an absolute sucker for a certain kind of bribe. Back then, for some reason or other, I was always interested in playing with toy soldiers. In those days, they cost a nickel apiece at the 5&10 cent store. (Yes, you young readers, you missed out on that great institution, the "Five and Dime" stores.) Anyway, to entice me to go into NYC for a modeling job, I was told that I could have a "whole" dollar after the photography session… I took the bait every time. When the "shoot" finished, we always headed straight to the store to buy 20 more toy soldiers. I had a collection of toy soldiers that defies description.

Another perk on those trips into NYC was to go to a Horn & Hardart's restaurant for lunch. That was a chain of inexpensive restaurants throughout the city that featured food displayed behind little glass window boxes. There were slots to put nickels in, and when the correct number of nickels was inserted, you could then lift the glass door of the box and remove the item.

Then too, the beverage was always fun to get. They had spigots mounted in the wall, in the shape of a Lions head. One placed the glass under the Lions mouth, put in a few nickels in the slot, pulled a lever, and presto, milk would pour forth. For me, my favorite Lion was the one that dispensed the chocolate milk.

I was hooked on always having a ham sandwich, a side order of creamed spinach, and chocolate milk. I don't think I ever varied my selection. But the real fun was putting the nickels into the slots and have things happen. (Do you suppose that's why I can't pass up a Vegas Slot Machine to this day?)

Later on in the book, I'll tell you a fun story concerning the Horn & Hardart restaurant …and two regular customers who became very famous later on in their lives. Walter Matheau and Dick Van Patten. Oh Heck! I might as well digress and tell you about it now. At my age, I'll probably forget if I wait until later.

It seems that both Walter and Dick were, from an early age, what some people might call "Compulsive Gamblers". We know that for certain about Walter and his propensity for gambling, particularly the "Ponies". I wasn't aware at the time that Dick Van Patten, in his misspent youth, shared Walter's interest in gambling… but here's the story that I was told.

As with most actors early in their careers, it was either "A Feast or a Famine" when it came to getting work. At this period in their lives, I'm not sure if they were both gainfully employed, or just hanging out together in-between auditions, and casting calls.

It turns out that one of their favorite hang-outs was a Horn & Hardart located on Broadway. (Do you suppose that they enjoyed putting nickels into the slots like I did? Did that contribute to Walter's reputed gambling addiction?) In any case, as the story goes, those two would bet on almost anything. So, as often happened, while sitting in this Horn & Hardart, to kill time, they

5

would take turns furiously spinning the "Lazy Susan" located in middle of every table that contained the condiments. Betting each time on where the catsup or mayonnaise would end up. I'm not sure what the wager was. Probably the loser had to pay for the coffee! I can just picture those two characters sitting and spinning, betting up a storm.

I never had the pleasure of working with Walter when I "graduated" from modeling and became an actor, but Dick and I did a number of radio programs together.

Ok…back to my getting "perks" for modeling jobs. (Buying toy soldiers and Horn & Hardart nickel "slots".) I mention all this primarily to show that I had "fun" working. I don't recall it being a grind. My parents made sure I was never overtaxed or became too tired if the shoot was time consuming and difficult under the hot lights of photography studios.

But this "forced child labor" (just kidding) didn't happen because my Mother woke up one day and decided that her freeloading youngster should get out and earn living. It happened quite by accident.

The story goes that when I was about 2 years old, while my Mom was walking me in a stroller one day, some woman came along and "gushed" over me, saying what a beautiful baby, etc. And that I'd make a perfect child model. (Now, what Mother wouldn't be influenced by such nice things being said about her Son?)

But as it turned out, this woman also knew a little something about how to get started in the modeling business, and explained how to go about getting composite pictures made, taking them to agents, etc...... and the rest , as they say, is history.

I think it is also significant to note that back in those days, practically all product advertising was almost exclusively done in print. Magazine Ads, Catalogues, Billboards, (even Newspapers) provided a steady stream of work for Models of all ages. (My Toy Soldier collection grew by leaps and bounds.)

I honestly don't recall details about all the photographic sessions that I was hired to do. But my folks kept an extensive scrap book of ads, magazine covers, etc. that they cut out and pasted in the book whenever they came across them. The scrapbook shows pictures from over 100 modeling assignments, but I probably did 4 times that many over an 8 year span. The book only contained ads that my parents found in the various print media that they happened to read.

I believe the picture on the following page was the first modeling assignment I was hired to do. It appeared in a New York newspaper, but I have no idea which one.

Believe it or not. It was for Macy's *Norwegian* Cod Liver Oil.

What the heck is a smiling kid doing selling that product. UGH!

Was the caption below it……"Hey Mom… That's yummy…

Can I have some more?"

For some stupid reason, that vile stuff was in vogue back when I was kid. My Mom had to hold my nose to get me to swallow a tablespoon of something that only an Eskimo could love. It was supposed to be good for you. Undoubtedly a rumor spread by the Norwegian Cod Fishing industry.

Other "medieval" tortures inflicted on us kids from that generation were… Castor Oil, Milk of Magnesia, and the infamous Mustard Plasters. Thank God for Modern medicine.

Looking back at that scrapbook now, I can definitely recall some of the events and circumstances surrounding many of the modeling jobs. Particularly those that were fun to do. I can categorize them as the four T's…"Thrills, Treats, Tasks & Trauma's."

For example, I recall a shoot that we did somewhere in NY State where the legendary wild animal trainer Frank Buck maintained a tourist attraction. I got to meet this famous Lion Tamer, and even play with one of his lion cubs. Big "Thrill" for a kid!

A "Task" definitely would be having to wear very heavy clothing under hot studio lights.

Shooting Snow Suit ads for catalogues was usually done in the summer, far in advance of the season. Notice the absence of a smile on my face.
(PHEW!)

9

A "Trauma" was definitely the time I had to pose totally naked in front of some strange lady. I was quite modest at that tender age. (But happy to say, I outgrew it later on). You have to admit however...A cute Butt, right? (Ok! Ok!..." was" that is!)

It bugged the hell out of me that the other kid in the shot at least got to have a towel wrapped around him.

A "Treat" or fun job would be to have someone put clown makeup on my face for a Magazine Cover photo. As I recall, we did this shot on the rooftop of the building that housed the photographer's studio. A cost saving to him by not having to transport and set up his equipment someplace else.

Can you believe the price of the Magazine?

11

Below is an example of one of my early "composites" that the modeling agency supplied to all the major photography studios throughout NYC. Child models had to have these composites made frequently, so the pictures would accurately reflect what the child currently looked like, and keep pace with the kids maturation process. The John Robert Powers agency was the one that most photographers trusted to deliver the "face" or type they needed to fulfill their assignments from the Advertising Agencies.

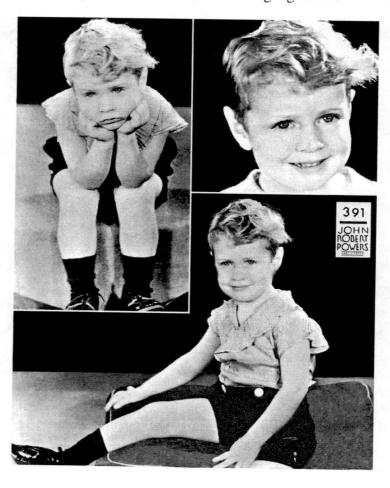

It also looked good on my modeling resumé to be able to say I posed for some of the really famous commercial artists and photographers of that era. Photographers Victor Keppler and Otto Hesse to name just two. I guess they found me easy to work with, and I found them fun to work for.

A lot of "shoots" were a piece of cake. Like the one where all I had to do was lay in bed (obviously a sick child) with only my hand sticking out from under the covers.

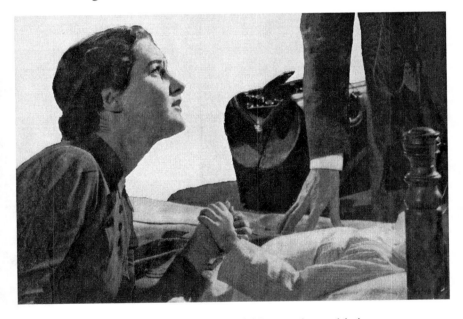

As the saying goes...I could have phoned it in.
($10 bucks an hour for this?) In 1938, that was a fortune.

But more often than not, I never knew what use would be made of the pictures that were taken. I did some weird costume shoots that would be "pasted up" by the people in the Ad Agency art departments for any number of products or services.

I wasn't always holding a product, with a big smile on my face.

They could come up with some of the weirdest outfits to dress us in. I often felt silly with the dumb things I had to wear.

But for every stupid costume I put on, I got the chance to dress up as a cowboy or Indian often enough. That was fun!

Then there was one assignment that I was sent on that probably resulted in my **biggest** exposure. In size as well as frequency.

I often posed for the famous artist illustrator, James Montgomery Flagg. In this instance, he was commissioned to do an illustration for a Traffic Safety campaign sponsored by the NYC. Police Department. It wound up on huge billboards all over the "Big Apple".

Although my face was not recognizable as such, I got a big kick out of seeing myself on those huge billboards. And no...I didn't go around tugging on peoples sleeves saying, *"Hey! That's me up there"!* But I did take some quiet satisfaction knowing I really hit it big. (Pun Intended).

If memory serves me correctly, (after all these years), I think I did far more product ads in the 1930's, than catalogue work. And many of those companies and brand names exist to this day. Heinz, National Biscuit, G.E. , Goodrich, Schick, Wrigleys, Corning Glass, Post Cereal, etc. In retrospect, I sure wish I had been paid with shares of penny stock in those companies rather than cash.

But I can say without too much fear of contradiction that I was not a conceited child. My folks would have paddled that out of me for sure. I was raised to be polite, courteous, and well mannered. *"And don't you forget it young man"* was heard often from my folks in those formative years. They didn't take any crap from me. Consequently, I didn't grow up to be a spoiled "Show Biz" brat. However, I wasn't all that passive or humble either... Let's just say I developed healthy self confidence. Fortunately, I carried that with me as my performing career developed, and when I branched out into TV Directing later in life.

Let's finish up with the Child Modeling career, and get on with the story.

The way that profession worked was; whenever a photographer or illustrator needed someone for a project, they would contact the Modeling agency, describe the type they were looking for, receive a few composite photographs of models fitting that description, and then make their decision.

Eventually, the Powers Modeling Agency decided to concentrate solely on Female models (Print and Fashion Runway), because they were in the greatest demand. They stopped representing male models. However, since I was always a little money-maker for them, they retained me as a client, and I kept busy over the years. As more and more photographers and illustrators became familiar with my face and learned that I was "easy" to work with, and very professional, they simply called the agency... checked my availability, and booked me. The agency then notified my parents of the time and place.

But it should be noted that the photographers themselves didn't necessarily have the final word as to what model they hired.

The "creative" people from the Advertising Agencies had a great deal to say about it. Usually, the Ad Agency Art Director had the ultimate responsibility for the print ad, and the end results could make or break careers. (Their careers, I mean.) The pressure on Agency people was enormous. (And even more so today, with the bigger bucks and TV ad budgets involved.) The finished product always had to please the top brass back at the Agency, and most importantly, the "Dreaded Client".

The Advertising Agency business back then, and to this day, is a very stressful industry. The creative people involved either produced successful ad campaigns, or the client took his advertising budget elsewhere. It is truly a very paranoid and competitive way of life.

Generally, the <u>successful</u> photographers were the ones who made the Agency Art Director look good. The <u>successful</u> models were the ones that made the photographers look good.

More often than not, the photographers were not given a great deal of creative freedom. It was their job to faithfully reproduce the layout given to them by the Art Director. And one dared not deviate from the "layout". Layouts were like a blueprint of what the finished ad was supposed to look like.

In most cases, it was a rough sketch of what the human figure would be doing in the ad, with the copy pasted on to show the headline, logo, and overall design of the proposed advertisement.

The layouts, (in varying degrees of artistic detail) had to be initially approved by the Agency Creative Supervisors, and the Agency Account Executive (who was the contact between the client and agency creative personnel). Once they got all their ducks in a row, they then had a meeting with the client and showed him the large layout for his final approval. To this day, these Ad Agency meetings are frequently called "Dog and Pony Shows". Don't ask why! I guess they likened it to the Circus Act with ponies running around in circles, while great numbers of dogs scampered back and forth, hopping on and off the ponies backs. Mass confusion and frenzied activity.

At these meetings everybody had to sign off on the concept (as being finally approved), and then it became the Art Director's job to select and hire the photographer to shoot the actual scene.

Needless to say, very few photographers dared deviate from the original layout. However, depending on the clout of the Art Director, and the degree of faith that the client had in him, he might have the photographer shoot variations on the theme (in addition to faithfully reproducing the approved layout), hopefully getting something better on film, and selling the client on the deviation later on....they called those "Happy Accidents".

But the Art Director always had the approved version to fall back on. It's called protecting one's ass. (That's an Ad Agency term that means trying like hell not to get fired).

On the following page is an example of the sort of challenge that often presented itself to the photographer. It this case… an ad for Crisco. (God knows what the copy was supposed to say). Very likely, about some kid "happily" running home from the grocery store with an important ingredient that "Mom" needed so she could bake his favorite cookies. Whatever!… The photographer would never have been able to match the Art Director's precise layout if he had to shoot the child actually running, so… they faked it.

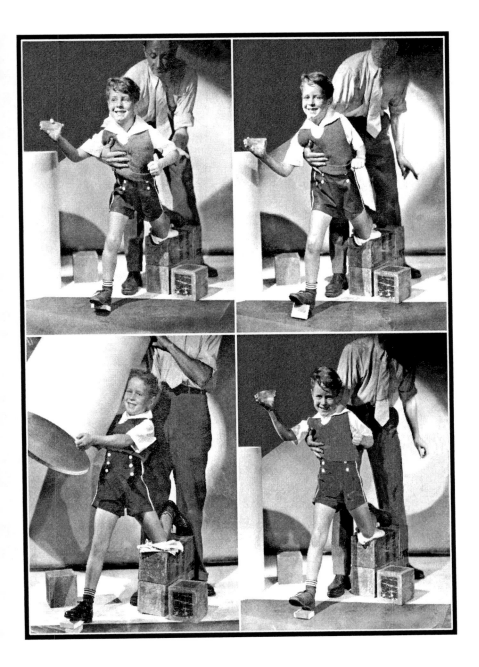

The wood blocks held me in a precise position (with some help from the photographer's assistant), and those props were removed later on by photo-retouching. Then, a "beauty shot" of the product put in my hand or arms by the same method.

So much for the brief walk down memory lane and the early modeling years. I'm just trying to outline the events and experiences that led up to my becoming an actor. Contacts were made, and a degree of sophistication was obtained that otherwise would not have been possible. I learned poise and self assurance at a very early age.

However, before continuing my "Show Biz" saga, I have a confession to make. Earlier, I mentioned my passion for playing with toy soldiers as a child. It was intensified even further when World War 2 came along in 1941. I was ten years old, and the war years created an overwhelming focus on things Military. The neighborhood kids no longer played "Cops and Robbers" or "Cowboys and Indians". We played all sorts of "War Games". Even obtaining surplus army equipment and uniforms to add to the realism.

That military indoctrination stayed with me all my life. It will be a recurring theme in this book, and I thought I might as well try and explain it now before going any further.

When I reached my teens, and was working in Radio, the 5 & 10 toy soldiers were no longer a lure. Oh No! I could now afford to upgrade to the more expensive (and far more detailed) "collectible" soldiers sold by F.A.O. Schwartz in NY. I even had friends who were into the hobby, and we'd do "Sand Table" battles in each other's basements. That went on until my late teens. And then... they were put away in favor of more fascinating "Pastimes".

Dating girls was more fun. But for some strange reason, they looked askance at someone who still played with, what to them, were "toys". What's that old expression? *"One can seperate the men from the boys...by the price of their toys"*. And girls sure ended up costing more than Miniture Soldiers. At least on a teenager's allowance.

Later on, when I attended college in the early 50's, (following military service in the U.S. Air Force), I became an almost fanatical Civil War history buff while studying that period. In the years that followed, it became practically an obsession. I read numerous books about it, painted battle scenes, sculpted action figures, and visited as many Civil War Battlefields as time permitted. (NOTE: for what it's worth. My Son was conceived at Gettsyburg.)

The Civil War Cavalry was always a major interest of mine, even to this day. Pictured below is a detail from a painting I did when I was about 35.

"Through Shot and Shell"

I eventually "graduated" from Civil War subject matter and became far more interested in the so called "Cavalry and Indian Wars", and was greatly influenced by the paintings of Frederick Remington.

For a period of time during my early days as a TV Director, I began buying unpainted Military castings, and would while away the hours using small brushes and a magnifying glass to create, what to me were, "Miniature Works of Art".

Working with my hands, either painting or sculpting, was always a great stress reliever. I could totally lose myself in the process and escape into another world.

These are examples of some of the 2 1/2 inch highly detailed minitures I painted around the early '60's.

I never understood my obsession with the Military, until all this recent Genetic Programming Research. I originally thought that I was simply brainwashed as a child, what with all the war movies, propaganda, game playing, etc…but as it turned out, it also was in my genes.

My Mother's two brothers were career Navy and served in both World Wars. Then, much later on in life, I discovered that I was related to an individual on my Father's side who fought in the Civil War, and was killed while serving with the Union forces at the battle of Gettsyburg.

Also, a relative of my Grandmother (on my Mother's side), participated in the so called Cavalry/Indian Wars. He rode with Custer's infamous 7th Cavalry, at the "Battle of the Little Bighorn". Fortunately, he was in Major Reno's detachment and survived that debacle.

Now, what has all this to do with a book about my career in Show Business? Nothing much, I suppose... other than the fact that I almost made a career of the Military...and I'd have had to write a whole 'nuther ending to this tale. Let's just say... wiser heads prevailed.

Enough of this digression. As my favorite movie hero, John Wayne often said..."*TROOPERS MOUNT! ...COLUMN OF FOURS" : HO!!!* as we gallop off into the future, in a Blaze of Glory. Straight into the acrid smell of the battlefield and the roar of the cannon. Sure!... in my dreams.

Actually...it was charging forward to "The Smell of the Greasepaint, the Roar of the Crowd".

Act 1

Scene 2

(Music up and under) "There's no Business Like Show Business"

(CUE NARRATION)

Now, we skip forward a bit. By age 8, I was considered an old modeling "pro". One day, on a photo session involving a bunch of other kids, the Mothers were all sitting around (off the set) and swapping gossip. Someone asked my Mother if I had been over to NY's Empire theatre yet, to read for a part in the new play they were currently casting. She said they were looking for red headed kids (of which I was one) for a stage play that was going to be titled "Life With Father".

Ah, the twists and turns of fate. It just so happens that I could read fairly well at that age, and had lots of experience following direction as a model. You know… look sad!… look happy!… look excited!…… and the whole gamut of visual expressions. To make a long story short, I auditioned for the play and was offered the part. That of the youngest child in the show, a character named "Harlan".

When my parents discovered that becoming a stage actor involved lots of rehearsal time (time away from earning big buck modeling fees), and that the salary they offered wasn't all that much (since the producers weren't sure it would be a hit), my folk's turned down the offer. I say again. Ah, the twists and turns of fate. As any of you show biz buffs already know, the play opened up to rave reviews and set the record for the longest running show on Broadway for a great many years to come. The original New York cast starred Dorothy Stickney and Howard Lindsey as "Mother and Father". (Lindsey was one of the plays co-authors and married to Stickney)

When the producers realized what a smash Hit Show they had on their hands they immediately began assembling a "Touring Company" to star the legendary actress Lillian Gish. And, as her co-star, Percy Warham. The producer contacted my folks again.

January 5, 1940.

Will you please come to the stage

door of the Empire Theatre on Monday, Jan.8

at2:15p.mto read for LIFE WITH FATHER.

Oscar Serlin Productions.

They sweetened the salary offer, and paid my Mother an additional $35.00 bucks a week for food and incidentals. Thus my Stage Acting career was launched. As were the show biz careers of a great many other youngsters. (I could probably write another book on that subject alone.) I'll spotlight some of those familiar "names" a bit later.

This particular stage play, (and its many touring or "road" companies), used up a lot of child actors over the many years that the play ran on Broadway and elsewhere. It was a grist mill for young talent who kept outgrowing their parts...having to be replaced by yet other youngsters, who in turn, would also eventually "outgrow their costumes".

Be that as it may, I was blessed with the opportunity to work with, and get to know intimately, that wonderful Film and Theatre Icon, Lillian Gish. Being childless, and never married, she somehow "adopted" me as her surrogate son off stage as well. To her, I was her "Baby Harlan".

Lillian Gish's theatrical career began in Silent Films in 1912, and she was still going strong in the Theatre, Films and Television 63 years later.

This is as good a time as any to mention how my Professional Acting name became "Harlan" Stone. I was born Harold F. Stone Jr. (named after the "Iceman" I mentioned earlier). But because there already was a member of Actors Equity (the Stage Performers Union) whose name was Harold J. Stone, the Union wanted my folks to select a new first name for me, to avoid confusion between the two "Stone" boys.

Note: Harold "J" went on to do a great deal of work in T.V. and motion pictures., usually playing a "Heavy". I couldn't go on to play "Heavies". I was too darn cute. (Yeah! ...Sure!).

Since my character's name in the play was "Harlan", my folks took the easy way out and stuck me with "Harlan Stone" as my professional stage name.

I HATED IT!!!. I thought it was sissy sounding.

Not that I liked the name "Harold" all that much to begin with. I would have much preferred being called "Tim" or "Brad", or something more macho sounding .

Of course, we also went through all the silly name choices for laughs. Like Curb Stone, or Precious Stone, or Key Stone. "Blarney" Stone would have been perfect, considering my Irish Heritage. In later years, when I had a son of my own, I wanted to call him "Rocky" Stone, but got voted down real quick. His Mother had no imagination. (Or was it no sense of humor?)

Enough of this levity. Back to my "new" career as a Broadway actor. Well... to be more accurate, perhaps that "new career" really began a tiny bit "Off" Broadway. OK!...OK!...so maybe it was more than a tiny bit "off", since the first stop on the play's tour was in the heart of the what was then this country's second largest city... Chicago.

But the cast never got any further than that. The show was a huge smash hit in that town as it was in New York, and everyone had to take up long term residence in the "Windy City". Well, to be more precise, I was only there for about 10 months, until I became too big for the part. After I left the cast and returned to New York, the show continued its run there at the Blackstone Theatre and set a new record for longest running play. (Almost 16 months). David Jeffries (my understudy) took over the role for me.

This Newspaper ad ran during the plays run in Chicago.

Here's Harlan*, youngest of the clan,
A happy, willful little man
Until he tries his oatmeal bon
in
OSCAR SERLIN'S *Production of Clarence Day's*

LIFE WITH FATHER

Made Into a Play by Howard Lindsay and Russel Crouse

Lillian Gish • Percy Waram

▶ Seats at the Box Office or BY MAIL for all performances

300 GOOD SEATS AT Every Performance **$1 10**

EVES. (Except Sunday) at 8:30. MATS. WED. & SAT. 2:30
Eves., $1.10; $1.65; $2.20; $2.75. Wed. Mat., 55c; $1.10;
$1.65; $2.20. Sat. Mat., $1.10; $1.65; $2.20.

BLACKSTONE
Theatre Michigan at 7th

* Portrayed by
Harlan Stone

Those cheap seats must have been for the 2nd balcony.
(And dig the costume I had to wear).

However, since this book is intended to be primarily about
my Radio career, I should casually mention that I did my first radio
show in Chicago in 1940.

The cast had obtained quite a bit of Celebrity Status with the success of the play, Also, the press agent, Wally Fried, sent us out on many promotional appearances. So, one day I was invited to be a guest on a popular interview talk show of the period.

```
MEMO MRS. STONE:


Harlan and Jimmy are to broadcast at 11 A.M.
Sat., June 29th.  With Elizabeth Hart. Station WMAQ.

If they will go to the studios of WMAQ, on the
20th floor of the Merchandise Mart, on Friday,
June 28th, at 2 P.M., Miss Hart will interview
them to prepare a script for the following day's
use.

She asks that they come an hour before the broad-
cast (10 A.M.), to run over the material before
they go on the air.  Don't forget, will you?

                                        HF
```

Many years later, while appearing in a different play in Chicago, "Tomorrow the World", I also made a guest appearance on "The Quiz Kids" program… another very popular radio show back then.

I think that the "Quiz Kids" producers probably might have prepped me ahead of time about the subject matter so I didn't look like a total imbecile next to those incredibly brilliant kids. They were the precocious "Nerds" and "Geeks" of their day.

At this point, I'd like to offer a few more insights as to the significant effect Lillian Gish had on my life when I was in the cast of "Life With father". Not only back then, but as of this writing.

The first thing I should mention was how kind and gracious she was to me, as well as to my Mother who accompanied me.

About a month after the play opened, I awakened early one morning with a high fever. By mid afternoon I became incredibly nauseous. The onset of what turned out to be acute appendicitis. The "Quack" resident Doctor from the hotel where we were staying was called to our room to examine me. He misdiagnosed it as a "Tummy Ache", and prescribed a laxative. (I told you he was a quack.) By the time I left for that evening's performance, I was in real bad shape.

I guess I rallied enough to get my makeup on, but my stomach was so bloated they had to "pin" me into my costume because the buttons wouldn't reach the button holes. I was throwing up all over the place, sick as a dog, and the Theatre Doctor was quickly summoned.

In the meantime, I'm being told by the Stage Manager all about the Show Biz creed, "The Show Must Go On". It seems that one of his duties during the prior month was to coach a local boy as my "understudy" for the part. As luck would have it, the kid wasn't quite ready, and didn't know all his lines. I was made to feel that if I didn't make it on stage that night, the show had to be cancelled, and the audience would have to get their money back. Another expression that was used back then was that a professional actor was expected to be a "Trooper" (or was it "Trouper"?), and rise above adversity.

Somehow or other, when the curtain went up, I managed to make my opening entrance. But when I left the stage they had cleared off a prop table in the wings… The Doctor placed me on it and monitored my condition constantly…while others pinned on my change of costume for the next act. By then, I was one very sick puppy.

Rather than be too melodramatic about this whole bit, suffice it to say I somehow made it through the performance that night, but had to skip my curtain calls because they had an ambulance waiting right outside the stage door. (With doors open, stretcher ready, motor running). They whisked me off to the hospital immediately after my final scene was finished. I was scared silly. I'd like to use another term, but I didn't know it back then.

I think the most frightening thing was that upon arrival at the hospital, with sirens blaring, they wheeled me into some "lab" type room to do blood tests, etc... and on shelves all along the damn walls were large glass jars full of all sorts of body parts. Like a lab scene in a Horror Movie. There I was, sick as a dog, in lots of pain, and I had to look at that scary display. I was terrified... crying hysterically, and listening to them talk about my needing an immediate operation. Ugh! And since I was no stranger to the smell of ether, I was shaking with fear at the thought of a mask being put over my face, suffocating me with that God awful smell.

It's amazing how some memories never fade, even after 64 years. But there is a happy ending. Obviously, I survived the experience. That was a definite plus. But I found out later that if I hadn't been operated on within the hour, the appendix would have "burst", and in those days, it could have been darn near fatal. Hell, just the thought of having to gag on ether damn near killed me. You "youngsters" (under 50) don't realize how lucky you are that they invented Sodium Pentothal and other really mellow anesthetics.

But the real fond memory I have of the traumatic experience was that when I came out of the anesthetic the following morning Lillian Gish was sitting at my hospital bedside, holding my hand. I guess my Mom had been up all night worried sick, and Miss Gish came by to relieve her so she could get a little sleep, or perhaps a bite to eat.

Lillian Gish was an angel. She visited me every day in the hospital until I returned to work a few days later. I felt as much love and affection from her as I did from my real Mom.

The second thing about her that had a profound effect on my life was the way she encouraged my artistic talent. As a kid, my folks kept me well supplied with coloring books and art pads so I could while away the time during lulls in my previous modeling assignments. This activity also kept me busy in my theatre dressing room when I wasn't needed on stage. When Lillian Gish saw some of my drawings, she made a big fuss over them, and offered to buy a few. I think the going price we agreed upon (based on size) was a nickel or a dime. I can only tell you, that by the time I left the show after almost a year, she didn't have any more wall space in her large dressing room, and I had a small nest egg.

That early encouragement from her as my first "art patron" influenced my interest in Art to a tremendous extent throughout my life. It almost became my Major in college. Although I didn't make it my career, it certainly came in handy when I became a TV Director and could express my ideas visually, design sets, do Story Boards, etc. I also used Oil Painting and Sculpting as therapy to unwind from the stress of TV Production. (But that's another book).

I have one other story about Lillian Gish that perhaps will give deeper insight as to how special she was. It happened many years later, and was one of the major highlights of my life.

Back in 1975 , I was firmly entrenched in my career as a TV Director in NY. But by then, I was a family man, with a son Harold, who was eight, and a daughter Debbie, who was thirteen.

That year , a musical opened on Broadway titled "A Musical Jubilee" that also featured Lillian Gish in the star studded cast. She had to be at least 81 years old by then. And would you believe? At that age, she actually did a charming little song and dance number in one of the scenes. I thought it would be neat to get tickets for my family, and take my kids in to see this legendary actress who had meant so much to me when I was a child.

Prior to the performance that evening, I prepared a sealed note to send backstage to Miss Gish via the Stage Doorman. In it, I said something to the effect that I'd be *"In the audience that night with my family, and if at all possible, could we come back stage after the show so I could introduce them to her."* I also mentioned that my son, who was with me that night, was the same age that I was when she and I first worked together in "Life With Father". I signed it… "Your baby, Harlan"… the name she used for me some 35 years earlier.

Following the performance, as we went down the stage door alley, it was almost impossible to get inside the door leading backstage. It was crammed with friends and fans of Miss Gish, all wanting to see this legendary icon of the theatre and silent films, and all anxious to express their love and admiration.

We finally made it to the near side of the stage itself, which was by then, wall to wall people. Way off, completely on the other side of the stage, standing on the first landing of stairs leading to some of the dressing rooms was Miss Gish, (so she could at least be seen by this adoring mob of people.) I had to lift my son up so he could get a glimpse of her from a distance.

Apparently, she had been there for quite some time before we even made it to our far off vantage point. She looked very frail and tired. After all, she was quite elderly by then. Her voice was faint, and only the people closest to her could really hear what she was saying.

Suddenly, her "Major Domo" (I forget his name) stepped up on the landing next to her and said in a loud voice (so the mob of people could hear), *"Miss Gish wishes me to thank all of you for coming to see her, and she's sorry she can't greet you all......But she's very tired and really needs to go to her dressing room. Thank you all again for coming"*.

At which point, her frail voice pipes up, carries across the width of the stage, and says...*"I'm not going anyplace until I see my Baby Harlan"*.

The Major Domo then stood up higher on the stairs to survey the crowded stage and yelled loudly, *"Is Harlan Stone here"*? I waved and yelled back from far across the stage, with a lump in my throat......*"Here"*!

(I must confess, I always get lump in my throat whenever I recall this event...and moist eyes.)

What happened next really blew my mind. The mass of humanity on that stage parted in the middle to let us pass. I now know what Moses must have felt like when the Red Sea parted before him.

The four of us walked triumphantly across the stage in front of hundreds of envious eyes. We finally reached Miss Gish, and as we hugged, she whispered, *"Lets all go down to my dressing room where we can talk and visit"*.

We didn't stay long, because I knew she was tired, and my main purpose for being there was to have her see and meet the great family that her "baby" had acquired. Her surrogate "Grand Children" as it were. It was a private and delightful moment.

And a fun thing happened on the way out of the theatre. The Stage Manager had remained behind (upstairs on the stage level), so he could escort us out of the darkened theatre. The only illumination was what we call a "work" light, a bare light bulb on a stanchion in the middle of the empty stage. The stage manager took my son's hand, saying, *"Here. Hold my hand. I don't want you tripping on anything*". When he reached the exact center of the stage, he stopped, let go of my Son's hand and said… "*Can you do this?*"… With that, he did what tap dancers call a simple "times" step. Sort of "Step" with one foot, "Shuffle" with the other. Then "Step"-"Step".

My son looked at him quizzically, then turned and looked at me with a "What the hells going on" look. So I said "*Go on, you can do it*". "*Watch, he'll show you once more*".

At which point the Stage manager repeated the tap sequence, and my son did his best to copy the tap dance steps. Then, the Stage Manager grabbed his hand again, pointed out in the direction of the darkened audience seats, and said as he gaily began walking across the stage again. "*NOW , WHEN YOU GET OLDER, YOU CAN TELL EVERYONE THAT YOU DANCED ON THE BROAD-WAY STAGE*". What a night!

I spoke with Miss Gish on the phone a few times in the years that followed, whenever our paths crossed geographically.

The last time I saw her was in the early 80's. I had already retired from my TV Directorial career and was living in Florida. She was in the area attending a retrospective of her work in films. I found out about it quite by accident, called the Theatre to see if I could reach her, and was able to leave a message.

A few hours later she returned my call. She had very little time on her crowded schedule, couldn't come to my place for a visit, so I took a quick run over to the theatre to chat with her briefly. I'm not sure, but I think that her seeing "Her Baby Harlan" reaching early retirement age may have been a bit unsettling. But she still had the spirit, good grace, warmth and charm that I will remember all my life. That was the last time I saw her.

Lillian Gish died in 1993. She was 99 years old. She lives on in the hearts and minds of many people. She will live on in mine forever.

CHICAGO

Dear Mrs. Stone:

I want to tell you once again how happy I have been playing with Harold.

He is an extremely talented child, with a very sensitive and kind nature. I am sure if you want him to go on in the field of acting, with a little care, he can be trained to play any part he can look.

I am sorry nature has taken him out of his babyhood as I loved having him as little Harlan in "Life With Father" these past ten months. He is such a little gentleman he will always be close to my heart.

All success, happiness, and health to you both.

Most earnestly,

Lillian Gish

November 12
1 9 4 0

Lillian Gish, and her Sister, Dorothy, both had outstanding careers in silent pictures. Lillian's name will be inexorably linked with the famous Director of that period, D. W. Griffith.

But her massive amount of film credits from those early days are only a small part of the story. She continued to amass many more credits in the legitimate theatre and easily made the transition to the "talkies".

More than any other actress that I know of, she brought to the profession a sense of grace and dignity throughout her long life. Her formidable talent was only matched by her gentle, kind and gracious manner. Put her picture in the dictionary next to the words "Sweet", "Charming", and "Dedicated".

I would imagine that by now, you get the message. Lillian Gish was my Patron Saint. She did more for my comfort level as a young child in Show Business, than any other individual I could name. Add to that, the incredible encouragement that she gave me regarding the development of my artistic talent. Consequently, the career path I took in Show Business definitely had the foundation laid by that incredible woman.

Come to think of it, there would be no reason or motivation to write this book, much less create the drawings that are included, were it not for the early encouragement that she gave me.

I mentioned earlier that the play "Life With Father" spawned a great many theatrical careers. Following are some names, (and where possible, photographs) of actors/actresses that went on to notable careers in the entertainment industry after appearing in this famous play.

I refer of course to the "Young" people in the cast. The character names of the four sons, and approximate age range, were as follows; "Harlan" (8), "Whitney (12), "John" (16), Clarence (20).

In addition, there was a young female character named "Mary" (the romantic interest for eldest son Clarence), and a key role in the pivotal "young love" subplot .

Richard Ney   Teresa Wright

In the Broadway production, I seem to recall Richard Ney was the original actor to play "Clarence". He went from that role to a notable career in films, appearing in about 14 motion pictures, as well as a number of TV Guest spots from the late 40's to early 60's. He eventually quit the business and had success writing best selling books about investing and finance.

Teresa Wright made her professional acting debut as "Mary" in this play. The incredibly successful career that followed is well documented. I could devote an entire book to her life and accomplishments, but someone most likely beat me to it. Would you believe she earned three Academy Award nominations for her first three films? And won the "Oscar" for Best Supporting Actress for one of those three in 1942. And, if that's not enough... two of the films she appeared in received the coveted "Oscar" for "Best Picture". She amassed over 41 motion picture credits, and guest appearances on over 20 TV dramas. Of all the "Life With Father" graduates, I'd have to say she leads the pack as far as awards go.

Now, you might well ask, what is a picture of that famous actress Greer Garson doing here?

No!... She was not an alumni of Life with father. But there is a fascinating bit of Show Biz trivia that connects her very closely with Teresa Wright... and even more closely to Richard Ney.

It seems that the famous wartime movie "Mrs. Miniver" (for which Greer Garson won the Best Actress Award back in 1942), also had as co-stars, Teresa and Richard. Ney played Mrs. Minivers son... Teresa played his love interest. Teresa's stellar performance in that film earned her a Best Supporting Actress nomination, and ultimately, the Oscar in that category. "Mrs. Miniver" also won the Oscar for "Best Picture" . Walter Pidgeon ("Mr. Miniver") was also nominated for "Best Actor". The only thing Richard Ney won for appearing in "Mrs. Miniver", was Greer Garson's hand in marriage. (She was about 15 years his senior at the time.) I'd have to say it wouldn't be bad duty being married to that lovely and talented lady. But it only lasted 4 years.

41

I think it's interesting to speculate just how come two young people whose characters were romantically involved in "Life With Father", ended up performing together again in "Mrs. Miniver". Who was cast first, I wonder? Did that individual then suggest the other one for the film? Or did Richard Ney get to know Greer Garson first, then suggest Teresa for the role she played? Hmmmm? Inquiring minds want to know. I sure don't have a clue.

O.Z. Whitehead   Andria King

O.Z. Whitehead also played the eldest son "Clarence", but in the same Chicago cast that I was in. He went on to play some major supporting roles in film and T.V. Notably, appearing with Henry Fonda in the film, "The Grapes of Wrath". I happened to see a "Mouldy Oldie" recently on TV... ("Road House" with Ida Lupino), in which he again played one of his "Goofus" characters.

I knew Andria King by the name of Georgette McKee back when she played "Mary" in our Chicago cast. She had done her first film "The Ramparts We Watch" in 1940, using her original name. Then, as Andria king, she did about 35 more films. Notably,

"Hotel Berlin" in 1945, and later played "Lillian Russell" in 1947's "My Wild Irish Rose". Andria also kept busy in TV, appearing on over 23 shows during her 50+ years acting career.

David Anderson, from the Broadway production, went on to play children's roles in NY Radio for quite a few years. David was quite a bit younger than I, and although I'd see him often around the halls of NBC, we never worked together. I'm not sure what he did in the business following his Radio career.

William (Billy) Redfield played an older son in the NY production, and had a lengthy career in Radio, TV and Films. One of his most notable Films was in a major supporting role to Jack Nicholson, in the critically acclaimed hit, "One Flew Over The Cuckoo's Nest". (More about Billy later).

Ted (Teddy) Donaldson eventually had a great role in film as a child actor, playing the young lead in Norman Corwin's film "Once Upon a Time", starring Cary Grant. Ted tells the story that in his later years, when graduating from Hollywood High, Cary Grant unexpectedly showed up at the ceremony to acknowledge the event and help Ted celebrate.

Now… that's a class act. (Pun intended)

Peter Griffith went from N.Y. radio into a production career on the West Coast. Then, met and married Tippi Hedron . Guess what?...That wonderful and charming actress Melanie Griffith is their daughter. What's the expression? "Apples don't fall far from the tree". In Melanie's case, the apple had to have been the "Delicious" variety.

Walter Kelly played "Whitney" in the NY cast. Went into films and TV later on. He appeared in his first film "The Well", in 1951, then acted in a few others. Was a dialogue coach for "Once a Thief", and in later years, appeared on TV in episodes of "26 Men" and "Perry Mason" .

In NY, Richard Noyes played the 3rd oldest son, "John". I'm not sure if he did any radio work, but his credits include a 1942 film "Junior Army" and some TV performances. Notably, "The Chevrolet Tele-Theatre. There is no indication that his acting career contin- ued after 1949.

Richard Simon from the NY Cast went on to a successful career as a Producer of Feature Films in Hollywood.

Larry Robinson from the NY cast performed on many Radio programs. (Larry and I worked together often.) He then went on to play "Sammy", a featured role in the "Goldbergs" TV series, and as TV's "Mac Foyle" in "Kitty Foyle".

Peter Jamison had a lengthly career just playing in "Life With Father". He first appeared as "John" in the Chicago Company, and stayed with that part for the duration of the run in that city. (16 months). Then, he apparently came back to New York and began playing the oldest son "Clarence" as a member of the Broadway cast.

William Daniels, a face and name that will be familiar to many of you readers, had a highly successful career. His connection with the NY cast of "Life With Father" was as an understudy for the older boys, and Assistant Stage Manager. He was born into a theatrical family and appeared on some early Radio programs as a youngster, including "The Horn and Hardart Childrens

Hour". In addition, as children, William and his sisters had their own Radio program called "The Daniels Family".

As William Daniels matured, he did a ton of work on the Stage, in Films and TV. His theatre credits include "Cat on a Hot Tin Roof", and the hit musical "1776". Some of his major film roles were in "Oh God", "Two for the Road", "The Graduate" and at least 15 other memorable motion pictures. His TV credits are numerous, and he will be remembered by many for his 6 years playing Dr. Mark Craig on "St.Elsewhere". He has won two Emmy Awards. Until recently, he served as the President of the Screen Actors Guild. You'll certainly have to admit...one of the busier members of the "Life With Father" fraternity.

I just recently learned something in conversation with Bob Hastings, my good buddy and long time "Archie" program co-star. Why I never knew this bit of information is beyond me. But it only goes to illustrate my point even further. Lots of **very successful** Show Business careers had their start with "Life With Father".

In this case, it has to do with Bob's younger brother, Don Hastings. Donald also played the part of the youngest son for about two years, then played the next oldest son for yet another year. That play ran forever! (Don was in the National Touring Company.). I have no idea what he's doing playing the trumpet because the part didn't call for it. The photo was probably the work of the "Life With Father" Press Agent. As for Don's early radio career, he was on NBC's Saturday morning kids show, "Coast to Coast on a Bus", as a member of that program's "Bunny Bus Chorus".

He was also in the stage version of "I Remember Mama" on Broadway. When Live TV came along, Don landed a plum role. For six years he played the "ranger" on Captain Video, an early space adventure program aimed at the younger set.

BUT! This floors me. Later on, he had a run of 4 years on TV's soap opera, "Edge of Night". This was immediately followed by 42 years of playing "Dr. Bob Hughes" on the TV soap "As the World Turns". YIKES! <u>42 YEARS</u> IN THE SAME PART... AND STILL GOING. And I'm happy to report...Success has not gone to his head... (Just his wallet).

Now, the beautiful young girl shown here was not in "Life With Father", but if the truth be know, she was undoubtedly the key element in launching the career of another child actor who joined the NY cast, (and also went on to enjoy great success in Show Business over many years). Her name was Berna Ann Cooper, affectiontely known as "Bunny".

When I returned from Chicago after playing "Harlan", I resumed my "normal" life, and went back to attending the local Catholic grade school. But Lo, what to my wonderous eyes did appear, but a new girl in our class. I was smitten. I was floored. I was to suffer from the worst case of Puppy Love and School Boy Crush the world had ever known. (Can you blame me?) To make a long story short, our families (Bunny's and mine) got to know each other fairly well.

When my Mom met Bunny's younger brother, Ben, she told Mrs. Cooper that he'd be perfect to play the youngest son in the Broadway cast of "Life With Father". So, I coached him a little bit in the part, (it gave me an excuse to go to their house and be around Bunny). He read for the play's Producer, got the part, and the rest is history. He took to acting like a duck takes to water. And he's still all wet!

Kinda cute, wasn't he. Ah, but his sister was even cuter.

48

Ben Cooper: Where do I start? He had a fascinating career in Show Business.(Radio, TV, Motion Pictures). He is a delightful character and one of my oldest friends. As a youngster in Radio, he logged about 3,000 appearances on various programs before heading to La La Land. (Our derisive term for Hollywood).

Ben and I practically grew up together. As it turned out, we stayed close friends (certainly longer than his sister and I did). I kept going out of town with other stage productions, and Bunny and I went our seperate ways...darn! All I had left to nurse my broken heart was Ben's friendship. And over the years, that has been extremely fun and rewarding,. I've watched him grow from a cute young kid to a cute cowboy. (I love zinging him!)

In the early 50's, Ben didn't hang around NY for very long. Following WW 2, we stopped playing "War Games" and went back to playing "Cowboys". But Ben decided to make a living at it. He went West, and started making Western movies. Just like that!

I guess he made about 30 films, and at least 25 of them were westerns.

He did his first film in 1950, and first western in 1952. Ben was put under contract by Republic Pictures, and had a pivitol role in his 7th film, 1954's blockbuster, "Johnny Guitar", playing the young wannabe Gunslinger, "Turkey Ralston". He was 22 years old then. Six films later, (1955) Ben traded in Western garb for a "Sailor Suit" and was in the critically aclaimed film "Rose Tatoo", starring Burt Lancaster and Anna Magnani.

Ben's love of horseback riding and pistols made him a natutral born Cowboy. He taught himself the "fast draw". (When one looks too young to vote, you had better be quick on the draw when the "Bad Guys" are coming to town.) But getting the gun out of the holster quickly means nothing unless you can hit your intended target. Ben became a crack shot, practiced constantly, and could "quick draw" in 1/5th of a second. He even taught Sammy Davis his fast draw skills.

Ben went on and did lots more western films, and a number of them with Audie Murphy. Remember Audie? He was the most decorated War Hero of WW 2, who became a western film star. But Ben's 30 films are only part of the story. He appeared on over 44 TV shows. Although his TV performance credits are heavy in the Western area, his all around acting ability showed through with roles on "Mannix", "Perry Mason", "Twilight Zone" , "L.A. Law" and other dramas as well. But it was the TV Westerns like "Zane Grey Theatre", "Bonanza", "Laramie", "Gunsmoke", and "Wagon Train" that kept Ben in the public eye…and "saddle sore" to boot, I reckon'.

However, while filming a "Wagon Train" episode in 1959, Ben's free spirited cowboy image got lassoed and hogtied.That's when that great Western star Ward Bond intro-duced Ben to the prettiest little gal he ever saw. Pamela by name. Shortly after that, her last name became Cooper. (In my opinion, the best thing that ever happened to him.) Pamela's  a living doll as evidenced by this recent photo of her.

The only sacrifice Ben had to make when he married Pamela was giving up wearing his Cowboy Hat and Spurs in bed every night. But Pamela's not cruel. She lets him keep his gunbelt on. He'd feel naked without it.

Hey Kid…That's the general idea! (Do I have to teach you everything)?

They make a great couple, have been two peas in a pod for over 42 years, and are two of my closet friends.

Although Ben is sort of semi-retired from acting, he still does his "Cowboy" thing. Each year, throughout the country, they hold many "Western Festivals", with all sorts of exhibits, contests, sales booths, etc. Many former Western Film & TV stars are invited. They sign autographs, and are interviewed in panel discussions for the benefit of all the fans in attendance. Some even participate in Celebrity Ride & Shoot contests. The object… to gallop down a zig-zag course in an arena, while shooting at balloons tied to poles. The Contestant rides like hell, and shoots at the balloons (positioned on either side of the course) with special paper wad blank cartridges. They use two six-shooters, (one at a time, of course) because there are 12 baloons they have to break. The rider who completes the course in the fastest time, and explodes the most balloons, wins the trophy. Usually a big Silver Engraved Belt buckle. My Buddy Ben, now approaching the ripe age of 70, won the trophy at such an event in 2001.

Joan Richardson, the young lady who has been such a big help to me in assembling and restoring many of the old photos for this book, made the following comment after seeing his pictures. "Gee…he's even cuter now than he was when he was younger".

Yikes! Shades of Dorian Grey!

That about wraps up the saga of what fate held in store for the Life With Father "Graduates". (I'm sure I goofed and forgot some, but you get the idea). All that remains is to clue you in as to what became of me after making my Theatrical debut in that play.

Although my "performing" career doesn't begin to compare to some of the others I mentioned, Show Business was good to me. I just took a different route.

Act I

Scene 3

(Music up and under) "Chicago, Chicago, What a Wonderful Town" etc.

(CUE NARRATION)

There were lots of positive things about being a Child Actor back in those days in Chicago. But there were definitely a few traumatic experiences (for an impressionable 8 year old) that I would just as soon not have had to contend with.

The neat stuff was all the perks. We were wined and dined all over town. I learned how to be the "perfect little gentleman" at cocktail parties, (and incredibly boring Social Teas). My parents believed in "Spare the Rod, Spoil the Child" so I learned good manners early on, and was always polite to my elders. It didn't pay to be a smart ass or get too big for my britches. Not that I was a saint. I managed to get into my share of mischief with other kids my age. We were in Chicago so long that I attended regular Catholic School there and had my share of school playmates. I also had my share of rapped knuckles from the nuns. A "Goody Two Shoes" I was not. Fairly normal under the circumstances.

I'd like to think I grew up with healthy self-confidence, but didn't walk around as if I was something really special. Having started so young as a model, by the time I became an actor, I simply looked at it as a just another job and not some lofty activity that people seemed to make such a fuss over.

To my regret, I don't remember all the wonderful and remarkable people I met at that age. And it was almost a nightly occurrence. Every evening after the performance, off came my costume and makeup and I was ready to go home to bed. (I hated having to use that "gooey" Maybeline). Then, the nightly ritual included a stop by Miss Gish's dressing room on the way out of the theatre for a good night hug and kiss. Invariably, she was still in costume, not having had time to change. Primarily because of all the notables that would be able to gain access to her dressing room after the show… to visit and pay their respects. I was always being introduced to all sorts of famous movie stars, classical musicians, artists, politicians, and anyone else who had the notoriety and "clout" to gain access to her on any given evening. But one person really stands out in my mind. I was awed by his reputation, having just read about him in my school history lesson. The famed Arctic explorer, Admiral Byrd. Wow!

A big deal for an eight year old. Unfortunately, I wasn't into autograph collecting back then, (or ever, for that matter). But I bet I could have filled many books.

Then too, there was a famous artist that Miss Gish insisted should see all my drawings on her wall. This gracious man took the time to give me some pointers, and sent me a box of oil paints to experiment with. Unfortunately, I don't remember his name… but I gotta tell ya, it wasn't bad duty being her "Adopted" Son.

The cast members of "Life With Father" were the Toast of the City, and as VIP's, we were invited everywhere. I recall this particular outing featured the entire cast, and had something to do with a major horserace. I believe that Percy Warham, Miss Gish's co-star, was an avid horse race fan, so he probably instigated it.

We even went to the famed Chicago Stockyards. Why I was dragged there I'll never know. I had nightmares after watching how they slaughtered the pigs. Not a pleasant experience. But it sure didn't discourage me from ever again eating ham sandwiches at Horn & Hardarts.

Living in a hotel was kinda fun too. A great diversion was the art of making water bombs. Some devious individual taught me how to fold a piece of typing paper (numerous times) so that it became a hollow "box" that would hold water. (But only briefly, until the paper got saturated). Once loaded, they could be dropped from any reasonable height, and on impact, explode and splatter water all over the place. Living on the eighth floor of the hotel was a more than "reasonable" height.

And as luck would have it, our hotel room window faced out on a busy main thoroughfare. Lots of pedestrian traffic also. Boy, did I ever get in trouble over that activity. (But I still remember how to make 'em, so stay out from under me).

Then there was a young bellboy named "Lucky" who became my buddy. If he was on duty, and I needed some excitement, I'd ride up and down in the elevator with him. If there were passengers who he knew wouldn't mind, he let me run it. I became quite good at stopping it level with the exit floors. It doesn't take much to amuse an eight year old. Besides, it was OJT (on the job training) in case my acting career went in the tank!

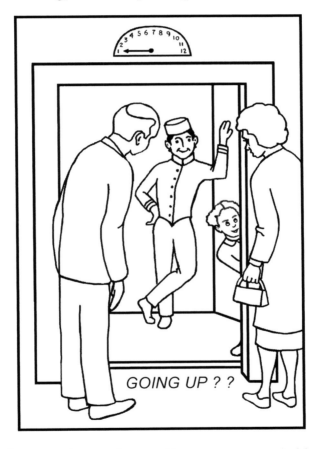

GOING UP ? ?

I realize now that my later radio career was probably plotted out for me there in that Chicago Hotel. (The Croydon Hotel, Rush and Ontario, if anyone cares to know.) It was probably demolished long ago. But it just so happened that two firmly entrenched residents of the hotel were a middle aged couple named Phil and Betty Lord. From what I recall, they were heavily involved in Chicago radio. (No, not Phillips H. Lord).

My Mother became very friendly with them. They sort of adopted the two of us, and I think that the things they told her about radio acting prepared her to launch me in that career as well when we eventually returned home to New York. But I hasten to add… she wasn't a "Stage Mother" who obnoxiously pushed her son into the business and dragged him all over creation to find work. As I recall, she'd find the right door, show me how to open it, but didn't shove or drag me through it. Guidance, not force, would probably best describe her technique and ambitions for me.

I guess it wouldn't hurt to mention a few of the traumas associated with being a child actor. One of them was the main reason I never wanted my children to get into the business. Too many weirdos to contend with. It's almost universally known that the creative arts attracts homosexuals. I have no quarrel with that, except if they happen to be Pedophiles. I was sexually molested by one of the older boys in the play, who lured me down into the basement of the theatre on the pretext of showing me something. He did. I won't go into the lurid details. He didn't remain in the part too long after that. I think he got caught with one of the child understudys that had to be on call every night.I met him many years later in New York, at a social function, and he was obviously heavy into the gay scene. Having put the abuse behind me long ago, I didn't slug him to even the score.

As an adult, I was well versed in the facts of life by then, and realized that the world is filled with all sorts of people. I learned I had to work with them. All I cared about was one's profession-alism. Sexual identity is a private issue, but I sure don't have much tolerance for Pedophilia.

Three other events were only slightly less traumatic to a young boy, but sort of humorous in retrospect. I mentioned earlier that I had red hair. I was a real "carrot top". Coincidentally, all the principal characters in Life With Father were supposed to be flaming redheads. The entire "Day" family, (Father, Mother, and all four sons) had to have red hair. Naturally, the producers never expected to always find redheads to fit the part, which simply meant that whatever actor was hired, they had to have their hair dyed with a Henna Mud Pack every two weeks.

Unfortunately, even though my hair was bright red, the stage lights "washed" it out somewhat, and it didn't match the vivid red/orange of the rest of the cast. So every four weeks I had to go to the huge "Hoity Toity" Beauty Parlor in Chicago's famous Marshall Fields Department Store, and sit for my Henna Pack. I was surrounded by nothing but females, (operators and customers), who would all be looking at me in the strangest way.

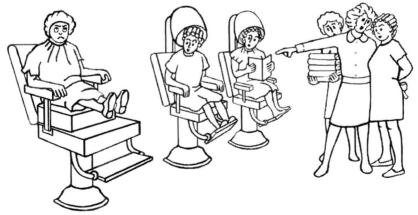

Looking back at it now, I can't say I blamed them. But I would have probably preferred drinking a whole bottle of Castor Oil (Ugh!) than have to endure all those stares, smiles, whispers and pointed fingers every month.

Then too, something happened on stage one evening, shortly after my initial First Act entrance. The scene called for the family to all be sitting around a large table having breakfast. (That's me in the foreground.)

My part called for me to resist eating my oatmeal, saying plaintively, "*I don't like Oatmeal!*" To which the Father very sternly demands that I eat it at once. Fearing Father's wrath, I am supposed to pour milk on it, spoon up a mouthful, and swallow it immediately. The Property Master stagehand was clever enough to use something other than oatmeal for each performance, and substituted Corn Flakes in the bowl. And instead of cream in the pitcher, good old Grade A milk was used. I LOVE MILK. So I had no problem performing that bit of business.

However, unbeknownst to me, a milk strike hit Chicago. The Prop Man substituted canned condensed milk in the pitcher. After pouring it on my cornflakes, I took a big mouthful, and immediately gagged when it hit my tastebuds. I then proceeded to spray cornflakes and foul tasting condensed milk across the table at my fellow actors, thinking I had been poisoned. Or even worse, ingesting thick spoiled rotten sour milk. Ugh! Were they ever surprised....but what the hell...So was I!

Another traumatic event in Chicago had an effect on me for the remainder of my life. Nothing earth shattering. But in a way, I'm glad that it occured.

It just so happened that our residence hotel was quite some distance from the Blackstone Theatre where the play was being performed. I'd guess maybe 12 city blocks. A delightful walk in the spring and summer. Impossible in the Windy City Winter .

In those days, sanity prevailed on our big city streets. And since the route to the theatre was along Michigan Boulevard, (a heavily travelled and very upscale throughfare) my Mother was comfortable with letting me walk to the theatre by myself on matinee days. It provided me with exercise and fresh air.

I could get there early and spend time playing catch or other games with the rest of the kids. Mom would join up with me at the theatre a little later on. (Photo from cover of local theatre magazine).
Note: I was the catcher. And throughout my youth (playing sandlot and organized baseball), I was always the catcher. I think the only reason I played that position was that I was the only kid who could afford the equipment. They call all that gear, "the tools of ignorence". How true!

But little did I realize that back then, that I was not normal looking to others passing by. Primarily due to my damned flaming red hair, and the fact that I had to let it grow very long, and parted in the middle. (That was the style in the 1880's, the historical period the play was set in.) Not to mention, I had very curly hair that was a real pain in the butt to comb.

Then too, my wardrobe didn't help any. It was summertime, and back then, young boys wore shorts and knee socks. Heck, knickers were barely out of style.

So here I am, traipsing down the Boulevard, hair flying in the breeze. (They didn't call Chicago the "Windy City for nuthin'.) During my stroll, I happened to pass two little old ladies coming from the opposite direction. No sooner had they passed, when I distinctly heard one turn to the other and say, in a loud voice.

"Look Mable! Did you see that?......Was that a little boy or a girl ?" I was mortified!

From that moment on, I hated having to wear my hair like that, and I vowed that as soon as the play closed, I was going to wear a crew cut for the rest of my life. No one else was ever going to mistake this 9 year old macho male hunk for a girl. No sir. Never again.

Authors note: At age 40, when Afros were the "in" thing, I sported a really good one, with my tight kinky curls. My associates called it the "Irish-Afro". I looked "cool" (certainly secure in my sexual identity by then), and was no longer concerned that someone would question my gender. But that day in Chicago, it was one embarrassed and P.O.'d little kid walking down the street.

However, that was not the worst of it. I had to wear what to me was a damned skirt in one scene.

In truth, it was actually a Scottish Kilt, but since I was of Irish extraction, it was a skirt as far as this "Macho Mick" kid was concerned.

And to add insult to injury...with a garter belt and stockings underneath.

I'm lucky I didn't grow up to be a cross dresser . It wasn't bad enough to have my gender questioned in public by two little old ladies, but to wear a skirt on stage every night was an even greater indignity. I discoverd later in life that "chasing skirts" was a hell of a lot more fun than wearing one.

That's my Dad getting me into costume, during one of his rare visits to Chicago.

I believe it was when he flew out from New York right after my appendectomy .

He somehow managed to get time off from his then job with the Postal Service and arrange for someone to take care of my younger sister Helen.

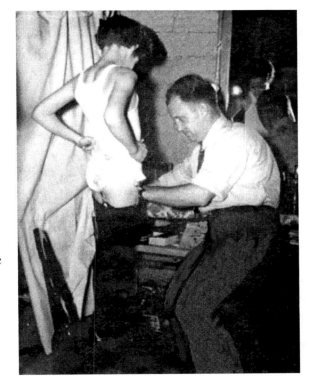

One final note about the long run of "Life With father". To sustain ticket sales, it wasn't enough to rest on the laurels of the rave reviews the play received in all the local papers after Opening Night. We had a great Press & Publicity agent named Wally Fried, who placed many paid ads in the local media, and made sure the play (and cast) got lots of free publicity by attending all sorts of activities around town. I'm not sure if we were compensated for doing those promotional stints. It may have been part of our contract. But no matter, we usually had fun, and were treated like Royalty wherever we went. but I usually insisted that I wasn't going to wear my "skirt" costume out in public!

The following pictures appeared in one of those "What's Going On About Town" publications that you frequently find in the better hotels.

Harlan Stone
"Life With Father" BLACKSTONE

Martha Raye, Jack Whiting, Ruby Keeler in Hold On to Your Hats" GRAND

You have to admit… heady stuff to have my picture bigger than that of the legendary funny lady Martha Raye….not to mention, the fabulous dancer of stage and film fame, Ruby Keeler.

While going thru the scrapbook , I came across this "Autograph Card" (following page). It was somehow or other tied in with a Kids Clothing sales promotion at Marshall Fields Department Store. It seems that all the "younger" kids in the cast (along with our understudys) were to show up at the store in costume for an autograph signing session.

Ah Ha! The light dawns! I wouldn't put it past the inventive Wally Fried to arrange for a trade-off with Marshall Fields.In return for our participation, I bet he arranged to get all the kids hair dyed for free in that Department Store's Beauty Parlour.

There were 4 regular cast members (the kids playing the 4 sons) and our three understudies. We seven were the only ones who had to submit to the indignity of the beauty parlour "dye job". But this time, the two oldest sons lucked out on this particular promotion. It was for the Young Boys Clothing department.

Percy Warham, the father in the play had it easy. He wore a red toupe. Miss Gish wore a wig, and used her real hair when she appeared "sick" in one of the acts.

BUDDY BUEHLER BRUCE PHILLIPS JACK
DAVID JEFFRIES HARLAN STONE PICCHIETTI

It gave us great pleasure to meet you at Marshall Field's

THE "LIFE WITH FATHER" BOYS

Shown 2/3 size

The understudy system was unique. I had my own understudy since none of the bigger kids could play my part. The next oldest had his own understudy. But... if the 3rd oldest got sick, the 2nd son stepped into the 3rd son's part, and "his" understudy subbed for him. The same musical chairs would occur if the oldest son became sick. Confused? Don't worry. The understudys rarely went on. We were fairly durable kids. (Except when it came to a unexpected appendectomy).

INTERMISSION

Veteran Theatre goers are very familiar with this tradition.

In The Legitimate Theatre, Intermissions served a very useful purpose. For one thing, it gave the audience an opportunity to stretch their collective legs after having sat for so long through the First Act. During the break, the theatre patrons went out into the lobby for either a cigarette (before smoking became such a no-no) or to purchase a cocktail or soft drink. (Very weak flavored Orangeade was popular back in the 40's). The audience was also offered an opportunity to buy Souvenir Programs of the play or musical, complete with lots of pictures of the cast.

Lucky you! You get pictures of the cast of characters that parade through this book without it costing anymore than the price of admission. At today's cost for souvenir programs, look at the money you saved.

But the Intermission often served quite another important function. It gave the "cast" a break to catch their breath, freshen their makeup, change costume, and also gave the Stagehands a chance to make any major scenery changes if required. Sometimes, entire sets were "struck" and new ones put in place. Generally, scenery changes were held to a minimum between the scenes of an act so as to keep the flow of the production moving along and not have long waits. The production was normally structured (written) so the lowering and raising of curtains between scenes normally denoted passage of time or perhaps as an "accent" to leave the audience in suspense, (A cliff hanger), or arouse their curiosity as to what could possible happen next. Assuming they even cared.

Many times, when the play or musical first opened, the Producer and Director usually hung out in the lobby during intermission so they could eavesdrop on the conversations that the audience members would be holding, (usually their reaction to the production so far), which gave them a feel for improvements that might be needed.

So! What do you have to say for yourself? Too late! Intermission over. Time to find your seat since the next act is about to start.

ACT 2

Scene 1

(Music up and under) "New York New York, It's a Wonderful Town, the Bronx is Up and the Battery's Down," etc.

(CUE NARRATION)

(With sarcasm) Yeah! Sure!... Can't help but comment about the New York of today. The "Battery" in that town is certainly not down. I'm of course referring to "Assault and Battery", not the Park in lower Manhattan. Back when I was a kid, all the city parks were havens for peaceful citizens, longing for open spaces and fresh air. Over the years, these parks became havens for muggers and druggies. I love living in Arizona at this stage of my life, having escaped all that nonsense. Out here, one can walk around with a six shooter on the hip. I'm not kidding. It does wonders for keeping "Crime" down to a minimum. Needless to say, I don't miss the "Big Apple". But I will admit Mayor "Rudy" had cleaned up the crime problems to a significant extent. It's much nicer now.

O.K. Back to my story. After arriving home in New York, my Modeling Agent was again contacted, and I went back to doing my modeling "thing". It was as if I was never away from it.

Fortunately, I had lost none of my "Boyish Charm". ☺

However, sandwiched in between modeling assignments and readings for other Broadway plays, a whole new world opened up. Auditioning for Radio programs of that period. It's strange, but the term "Casting Calls" or "Readings" was the term used for Plays... "Auditions" for radio... Go figure!

For this narrative, rather than jump back and forth between the two fields of entertainment that I was involved in during that period, I'll focus on my Theatre credits first, and get them out of the way. Undoubtedly, all of that stage experience and training stood me in good stead when I was getting involved with performing on Radio at the same time.

I think my next play (or plays) was for Regional Theatres. I did "Watch on the Rhine" (a wartime drama) for a brief period in two different cities, playing the young son "Bodo". I was probably about ten at the time. Since I had experience playing the part in one city, a different Producer hired me a month or so later for the other cast that was being assembled.

And then shortly after the run of that play, I was cast as "Michael" (the youngest of the Darling family) in "Peter Pan".

It was great fun being hooked up to "Fly" high above the stage. But there was a slight problem connected with that. (ooops. another pun!) The harness I had to wear dug into my crotch quite a bit, and often resulted in pinching and chafing some very tender spots, no matter how much padding they tried.

I'm surprised that I didn't enter manhood with an abnormally high voice. <grin> But for a kid, it sure was fun swinging above the stage.

I Flew'd!... I Flew'd!
(Ouch!! ~~censored~~ That Smarts!!)

I followed that with appearances in two "flops" on Broadway. "The Star Spangled Family" of which I remember very little and none of the names of the people in it. (It was about a war widow.)

I do remember that my character in the play was supposed to play the violin at one point. I had to take violin lessons from some old geezer who spit when he talked. I found that most unpleasant since he persisted in leaning in close to my face to show me how to finger the strings... a real drag.

I think I had almost mastered a few bars of "The Merry Widow Waltz", but for some reason the producers changed the instrument the my character was supposed to play, and switched it from violin to piano. (Was it because they heard my rotten violin playing?) Damn, if they had opted for the piano in the first place, I could have escaped getting all that spittle in my face, and my frustration with having to take lessons on such a difficult instrument. (The sacrifices we actors make for our craft!) ☺

As it was, I probably wasn't much better on the piano, but I guess one could at least recognize the tune. And thank God for small favors. The Piano teacher was a cute blonde, and didn't have a "juicy" speech impediment.

The Play opened and closed within a few weeks. Not all that unusual back in those days. Today, "mounting" a stage production costs so much that Producers almost have to bet on sure things. That's why there are so many revivals of prior successes. (Particularly the expensive musicals.) Anyway, I don't think they can blame the show's closing on my inept piano playing. At least I hope not!

Another play I appeared in lasted a bit longer, but also had a very short run. It was called "This Rock" and starred another legendary performer, Billy Burke.

The younger readers will not be aware of her early stardom, but all will certainly remember her as the "Good Witch" in the classic film, "The Wizard of OZ".

This play was also set in the War Years, and the plot dealt with British children being sent into the English countryside to escape the London Blitz. I had to develop a "Cockney" accent for that one. I was probably about 11 years old by then.

Two newcomers who went on to eventual stardom in Motion Pictures were also featured in the cast....... Zachary Scott and Jan Sterling. Unfortunately, Scott died at a very early age, just when his film career was blossoming. I always remember the actors and actresses that I performed with based on two criteria. One, obviously, was their talent. The second was equally important. How tolerant and nice they were to kid actors. The both of them get high marks in my book. Literally and figuratively. Ha!

That's me in the back, on the left side. And that pretty young blonde actress between Billy Burke and Zachary Scott is none other than Joyce Van Patten, the younger sister of Dick Van Patten (of Horn and Hardart lazy susan fame). Not to mention his fame as star of the TV sitcom, "Eight is Enough". Joyce herself went on to a notable career as an adult in films and television.

Usually, before a play opens on Broadway, the producers "try it out" in a city fairly close to New York. Places like New Haven, and Boston, come to mind.

I can remember when "This Rock" tried out, Jo Van Patten (Joyce's Mom), had to return home to NY, so my Mother looked after both of us kids on a temporary basis. Sometimes, if naps were required for us youngsters, Joyce and I had to share a bed in the hotel room. Careful now! (Remember, we were just kids!)

But I did have lots of fun at Joyce's expense many years later in our adult lives. We bumped into each other on a few occassions. If the two of us were with a group of people, I casually let it slip that I was the first male that Joyce ever slept with…… then watch her squirm out of it with hasty explanations.

I don't recall too much about Billy Burke. Obviously, I was very impressed that she played the Good Witch in "The Wizard of Oz". When I first saw the film as a young child, I can at least remember the early scenes she was in. But for the rest of the movie, I think I hid under the movie theatre seat when the Wicked Witch showed up. (Particularly the scenes when she sent the hordes of fierce flying apes to capture poor Dorothy and Toto). Speaking of "Dorothy" (the beloved Judy Garland), there's a story about her later on in this scene. (Or "chapter", if you prefer.)

But at the time of this play, Billy Burke was quite elderly, and more or less kept to herself. Therefore, she wasn't all that accessible off stage. It wasn't until I reached adulthood that I became aware of her stature as a legend with Ziegfield, and the Musical Theatre in general.

Another play I toured the USA with was a musical starring another Legend of the time, Gertrude Lawrence. The title… "Lady in the Dark". They later made a movie of her show business career, which starred the incomparable Julie Andrews. That film featured problems encountered when Gertrude Lawrence was preparing to do this particular musical.

WILLARD PARKER

HUGH MARLOWE

It also starred these two Gentlemen

79

Hugh Marlowe will be remembered by Old Time Radio fans as the original voice of "Ellery Queen", the Super Sleuth.

Williard Parker appeared in at least 46 films over his career and Hugh Marlowe, in addition to his radio credits, appeared in 37 films and appearances on 22 TV programs. Both of them formidable and popular actors of their day.

I mentioned earlier that the Actors Union wanted me to change my name to Harlan Stone, to avoid confusion with another actor of the same name. Well... both the above named actors also changed their names...but of their own volition. And I can't say I blamed them. "Willard Parker" was born Worster Van Eps. "Hugh Marlowe" was born Hugh Herbert Hipple. On second thought, wasn't there an actor named "F. Hugh Herbert"? Maybe Marlowe needed to change his name for other than the obvious reason.

"Lady in the Dark" was a lavish musical, produced by Sam Harris. The creators became legends on Broadway. Book by Moss Hart; Composer, Kurt Weill; Lyrics by Ira Gershwin. It was such an elaborate production, it could only play in theatres that could accommodate 3 revolving stages.

The story line had to do with a woman undergoing psychoanalysis, and each time she related a "dream" to the analyst, all sorts of stylized scenery "revolved" and turned to face the audience. Then lights would slowly illuminate the sets, and elaborate production numbers took place, representing her highly fanciful dreams.

There were lots of exotic costumes, and to fill them, lots of exotic chorus girls.

I hate to tell you what my primary recollection was about appearing in this lavish Musical with all these leggy and busty Chorus Girls. No...... Not that! Get your mind on a loftier plan.

THE CIRCUS DREAM

All those elaborate dancer's costumes were adorned with a gadzillion sequins and spangles . They became irresistible "collectibles" to the eight young children in the cast.

After each performance when the final curtain went down, all the kids in the cast would scurry around the stage like rodents to see how many of the bright "treasures" we could find that had fallen off the dancers costumes. Don't ask me why! It just seemed like the thing to do. I guess we were competing to see who could amass the most Baubles and Beads . At my age, it was more fun than spying on the chorus girls doing their quick costume changes in the wings. Besides, it saved the stagehands lots of time not having to sweep up all that stuff after each performance.

The roles that we kids played were children that the Heroine encountered when she also was a child. Fanciful Flashbacks to her childhood, dredged up during her sessions with her analyst. That's me in the window. The "Sultans" Sorcerer! Abracadabra! says I.

But I'm ashamed to admit something. I became good friends with the Wardrobe Mistress who was responsible for maintaining those lavishly festooned costumes, and on occasion, she slipped me some extra rhinestones and sequins. A lesson I learned early on in life. It's not so much what you know...but who you know.

The last theatre production I appeared in was another big hit. Another wartime drama titled "Tomorrow the World". (Circa 1942-44... in the midst of WW II). A very dramatic play about a Hitler Youth member (Emil), forced by his German family to come to America to live with relatives, in hopes he could be redeemed and be de-programmed away from his fanatical Nazi beliefs. A classic story of "Good" triumphing over "Evil". My childhood acting friend, Skippy Homeier, played the juicy part on Broadway, and went on to play the role in the motion picture version.

When the Producers eventually assembled the road show, I was cast as "Dennis", a minor supporting role, (and as understudy to the part of "Emil", the nasty Nazi kid). Dick Tyler had that role in our company. (As an adult, Dick went on to become a successful chiropractor in the LA area.)

Our cast had as the female lead, Elissa Landi, an incredible actress and lovely lady. Unfortunately, she died a few years after she left the play, so unless you're up on the careers of actresses from the late '30's and '40's, her name will probably not ring a bell. But to those who knew her, she was very special, and was much loved. Just like Lillian Gish, Miss Landi also did a great deal to encourage my artistic talents, helping me to develope and refine my art training, as you will eventually discover.

I mean...BIG TIME ENCOURAGEMENT!

To my private artist, Harold, with fond love and faith in his talent—
Elissa Landi

Georgous, wasn't she?   Elissa Landi had an international theatrical career, beginning on the London stage in the late 1900's, and in German films in the late 1920s thru 1930. She came to this

Country in 1931, and was one of the stars in Cecil B. DeMille's 1932 epic, "The Sign of the Cross". She appeared in about 20 Hollywood films, with her last one being the 1943 war film "Corregidor". As a matter of fact, I think she left our "Tomorrow the World" cast to appear in that film. Unfortunately, she succumbed to cancer 5 years later at the age of 44.

When Miss Landi left, she was replaced by Edith Atwater, who coincidentally, was married to Hugh Marlowe. A small world! If you recall, he was one of the leading men in "Lady in the Dark", the other play I previously appeared in.

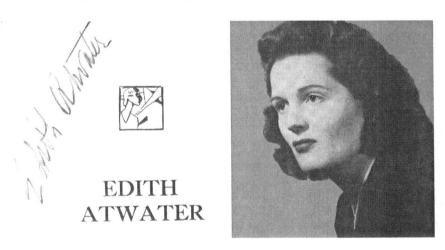

EDITH ATWATER

(Just think. Not only do you get photographs of these lovely ladies , but their autographs as well. And at no extra charge).

Miss Atwater did a lot of Regional theatre work, and had appeared in 6 other Broadway plays before being cast as Elissa Landi's replacement. Notably, she appeared in the mega hit, "The Man Who Came to Dinner", as well as "Springtime for Henry".

To demonstrate what a tight knit family the child actors of that period were, my younger sister Helen toured with us as the understudy to the female child lead. When our National Touring company finally reached Los Angeles, we had a reunion with the young star from the Broadway cast who was in Hollywood making the film version of that play, and other NY child actors.

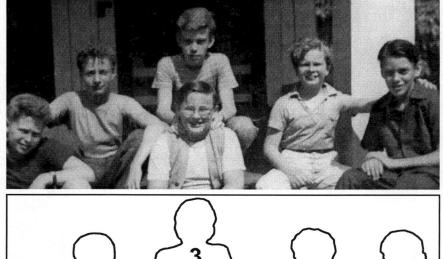

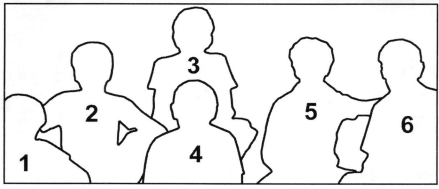

1) Dick Tyler (the lead in our touring company). 2) Yours truly. 3) Skippy Homeier, (the lead on Broadway, and star of the film version.) 4) Mack Twombly. 5) Ted Donaldson (Remember? He was the one in that film with Cary Grant.) 6) Howard Bixler.

Incidentally, also starring in our cast as the adult male lead, was a man whose name will be very familiar to Old Time Radio fans, Paul McGrath.

Mr. McGrath was famous for his portrayal of the sinister voiced host of that classic radio program, "Inner Sanctum" (The role also played by Raymond Edward Johnson.). Paul had an illustrious career on the Broadway stage in the late 30's and early 40's, as well as appearing on numerous Radio shows in the 40's. During the long run of this particular play, I came to know him quite well. I found him to be most congenial, warm, and a real "Class Act". He always seemed genuinely pleased to see me when our paths crossed in Radio many years later.

Interestingly enough, his equally charming wife Lulu May Hubbard was also in the cast, in a supporting role, playing the sister to Paul's character in the show. I throughly enjoyed working with the both of them.

While in "Tomorrow the World", I got to play that "Juicy" bad kid role a few times during the tour, and one thing stands out in my mind. Towards the end of the first act, "Emil" goes to his room (offstage) to change out of his traveling clothes after arriving in this country. He then re-appears in the unoccupied living room set, dressed in his Hitler Youth uniform.

Spotting the large portrait of his Anti-Nazi father high on the opposite wall, he pulls a library type step stool over to reach the portrait, removes his Hitler Youth knife from it's scabbard and proceeds to vehemently slash the portrait to pieces...... as the curtain falls...... a very dramatic cliff hanger.

If you recall, I mentioned earlier about my interest in things military. Naturally, with the war raging in Europe and the Pacific, the military was even more in focus for me.

I loved dressing up in that Hitler Youth uniform. At 12 years old, I was not conscious of the incredible evil that it represented. (Nor did the rest of the world back then in 1943/44.) I just thought I looked real "Sharp" in it . Blame my youthful naivete, but I thought that Germany's Hitler Youth organization was similiar to this country's Boy Scouts. Ironically, I was a 2nd Class Boy Scout at the time. More about that later.

To digress briefly, another uniform that I loved wearing even to a greater extent took place some years earlier. That of a Canadian Northwest Mounted Policeman. In the late thirties, Department Stores sold some really neat costumes. Cowboys, Indians, and Northwest Mounted Police. As a modeling assignment perk, I got the "Mountie" uniform. I think I practically slept in it.

I decided back then that when I grew up, I wanted to be a Mountie. Boy, was I pissed when I later discovered that you had to be a Canadian Citizen to wear that fancy scarlet tunic, boots & dark blue britches with the yellow stripe. Years later, when I was about age 40, I was invited to a Halloween costume party and finally fulfilled my fantasy.

As a TV Director, I had easy access to New York's famous Brooks Theatrical costume company. I showed up at that party resplendently attired in an authentic Mountie uniform. I put Nelson Eddy, Gary Cooper and Errol Flynn to shame. I was, except for an accident of birth, a Mountie at heart.

Enough trivial reminiscing. Back to the real world of Show Business. (Did I say "Real World"?) Ha!!!

While in the touring company of "Tomorrow the World", we played in a whole host of cities. And some of them were small enough to only warrant the infamous "one night stands".

The cast traveled across the country by train, while the scenery went by truck in many cases. It was a "one set" show, so it wasn't all that difficult to tear down and set up as we went from city to city. But being 13 years old, I missed out on seeing some spectacular scenery from the train windows. I usually had my head buried in comic books. ("Archie" comics had just come out.) But back then "Blackhawk" was my favorite. Again, the Blackhawk characters wore sharp uniforms. I was in a rut regarding uniforms I suppose. And as it turned out, never outgrew it.

"Tomorrow the World" played Philadelphia, Chicago, Minneapolis, Cincinnati, cities in Ohio, Oklahoma, Montana, Western Canada, and lots of places in between. I guess we were on the road touring for over a year, and ended up in California, playing in Sacramento, San Francisco and L.A.

Some interesting events occured while appearing in that play. Looking back on them now, I guess they were fairly significant, and worth recounting.

While enroute to California, (I was an old hand at train travel by then), my Mother (who always accompanied me), let me have free run of the train. That simply meant that I could go visit friends in other cars, go to the dining car by myself, and generally relieve boredom by moving about when I got the urge.

One day, upon entering the dining car, the waiter ushered me to a table where a young woman was already seated. Upon sitting down across from her, she looked up… said *"Hi!"*, and we started chatting. She was curious about my dining by myself, and I explained my Mom was traveling with me. She asked if I was going to visit relatives in California, and I explained that no, I was an actor in a play, etc. etc. To that she exclaimed that she was an actress as well, and we started to talk "shop" a little bit over lunch.

After desert, she asked if I knew how to play cards, (Gin or Knock Rummy in particular). Being brought up in Show Biz, I had already learned all sorts of adult card games to while away the time. ("War" and "Go Fish" were for babies.) So I said sure, I know how to play Rummy.

She brightened even more at that news, and asked me if I would like to come back with her to her compartment to play cards. I readily agreed, and we spent a fun afternoon playing Knock Rummy.

When I finally got back to my Pullman car, my Mom sort of scolded me for being away for so long and wanted to know where I'd been all that time. I explained about the young actress I met and our marathon card playing. When she asked the name of the actress, I blithely replied......Judy Garland. My Mom nearly had a stroke. Judy had recently starred in "Wizard of Oz" and was a household name. To me, she was simply another performer, a nice girl, and fun to play cards with.

Having grown up in the business, I was never awe struck by celebrities, and took the notoriety as part of the job. In later years, as a Director, I resented those performers who developed big egos and believed the press clippings that set them apart from other mere mortals. The mantel of "Stardom" can be worn lightly, or flaunted. Guess which one's were a big pain in the butt to work with?

Another event occurred while the play had a few month's run in San Francisco. Harking back to my fascination with Canadian Mountie's, we had recently performed in Vancouver B.C., and I got to see some of those sharp looking uniforms for real. One Mountie even put me up on his horse. (The perks of being in Show Biz.)

But a major international incident also occured in Vancouver, Canada.

All of the young boys in the cast of "Tomorrow the World" just happened to belong to either the Boy Scouts of America or the Cub Scouts. We had a sort of Troop / Den of our own among the cast members and Dickie Tyler's mother was our traveling "Den Mother". It was a unique situation, and the Publicity Director that traveled with the show would often use it in press releases.

Well……As it just so happened, there was a huge Canadian Boy Scout "Jamboree" that was ongoing at the time the show was playing in that area. In the spirit of international good will among the Scouting community, we were invited to appear as special guests before the thousand or so Canadian Scouts at their encampment.

I don't recall why, but I was the only member of the cast that could accept the invitation. So they sent a car to pick me up, and I arrived to a huge welcome. (Wearing my American Scout uniform, of course.) All the Canadian Scouts were assembled in a grassy amphitheater, facing a rustic stage. I was then escorted with great pomp and ceremony to the stage, and ushered into the presence of the Head Canadian Scout Leader, who was bellowing into a megaphone so all could hear, something like…

"And here he comes now. Our very special and famous guest from America., 2nd Class Scout Harlan Stone. As you all know, Master Stone is also a Broadway Actor, and is appearing in a famous play here in Vancouver, and he has taken the time to come visit us at this magnificent Jamboree. Yadda, Yadda, Yadda! Let's show this American Scout a real warm Canadian Scout Welcome".

All the Scouts are cheering, being lead in a "Hip Hip Horray" by the animated Scout Leader, waving his megaphone aloft, in tempo with the "three cheers". Then, in an act of conviviality, he claps me firmly on my back, and plunks the megaphone on my head to wear as a hat, much like a dunce cap.Unfortunately for both of us, what started out in fun and frolic, ended in disaster. The poor guy almost had a heart attack, and I almost ended up in a hospital emergency room. It seems that the metal "clip" that held the megaphone together had a very sharp edge. When he plunked it on my head, it split my forehead open. Riverlets of blood began streaming down my face as he looked on in horror.

Can you imagine what it's like when 1,000 Canadian Boy Scouts are eager to earn their Merit Badge for First Aid......It was a Chinese Fire Drill up on that platform.

Fortunately, they were able to patch me up so that I didn't require stitches, but I sure must have looked funny on stage that evening. It was a major problem covering the gash with makeup, while trying to avoid an infection setting in.

When the Company Manager and Stage Manager saw the wound, they gave me hell. I expected sympathy, since it wasn't my fault, but they only saw it from their point of view. If I had missed the performance that evening, it would have complicated the Company Manager's life no end. And Stage Managers also have enough to worry about, so they want the actors to stay healthy, and avoid mishaps and accidents at all cost.

When a play is touring, Company Managers have complete control. The play is turned over to them by the Producer and Director after everyone has been cast, rehearsed, fine tuned, costumed and sent out on the Road. It looks bad on a Company or Stage Manager's record if there are mishaps and screw-ups during the play's run.

I caught hell from him on one other occassion. One day he noticed I needed a haircut. Not necessarily for the small part I was playing, but in case I had to go on as understudy to the juvenile lead. That part required real short hair, (practically a crew cut).

So, I dutifully did as asked, and found a local Barber Shop in the "podunk" town we were playing in. I think it might have been Butte, Montana. (Sorry Butte, but back in the early 40s, it was "podunk" when it came to Barber Shops.

Towards the end of the haircut, I was sort of dozing in the chair when the Barber asked if I wanted him to use clippers on my sideburns. I innocently and blithly said "*O.K.*", not understanding what he meant.

In "Butte", I found out it means eliminate them. Completely! I was bald from the top of the ears down. When the Stage Manager saw me as I checked into the theatre that evening he gasped in horror. I certainly did look wierd.

For the next few weeks, I had to get to the theatre an extra 20 minutes early. It took much longer putting on my makeup each night, which now included carefully adding sideburns with an eyebrow pencil.

The play worked it's way down the West Coast, with extended stops in Portland, Seattle, Sacramento, and stayed for a much longer period of time in San Francisco (before continuing on to Los Angeles), and eventually coming to a close after a lengthy run in L.A.

One of the neat diversions I had during our long run in San Francisco was quite special. I met "Pepper". As a kid growing up on Long Island, I had learned to ride a horse, and went to the local rental stables as often as I could. I fancied myself fairly good at it. So, while in San Francisco, I prevailed on my Mom to rent a horse for me during our stay there. With the exception of matinee days, I went riding on "Pepper" along the Northern California coastline on a daily basis. (Naturally, daydreaming that I was a Canadian Mountie, galloping down the beach to rescue some damsel in distress.)

But no self respecting Mountie went riding without neat looking boots and jodpurs. So I set out to find riding boots just like those worn by the RCMP. One day, while walking through San Francisco's Chinatown, "Lo and Behold", there, in a cluttered shop window, was a used pair of riding boots that looked exactly like those worn by Mounties.

So what if they were size 12, and I wore size six or seven. The price was right, and by wadding lots of paper in the toes, I was able to happily clump along the street on the way back to our hotel room

It took many many years before I could wear them with less and less paper filling, and would you believe, I still have them in my closet today. And they are still a tad too big.

But that early interest in Uniforms and Horses was to stick with me for most of my life. Well, at least the Uniform part. There came a time in later years that I became less than enthusiastic about horseback riding. More about that later. But when it came to art and subjects to paint, I was already getting hooked on the calvary .

I previously mentioned that Elissa Landi (much like Lillian Gish), went out of her way to encourage my artistic talents. As it happened, the play "Tomorrow the World" had about a 6 months run in Chicago, and while there, I had a birthday. As a Birthday gift, Elissa Landi (who was still with the cast) presented me with a weekly Art Course at the prestigious Chicago Art Institute.

It turned out to be a lecture series, held in a large auditorium, and started out to be a trifle embarassing. I was seated in the balcony, and when the lecturer reached the podium, he began by announcing that there was a celebrity in attendance, mentioned my name, talked about the play, and insisted I stand and take a bow. That's not what I had in mind at all for my art training. Sitting in a lecture hall being stared at was not my cup of tea. Also, I found the lecture about the history of fine art incredibly boring. When I arrived at the Theatre that evening, Miss Landi summoned me to her dressing room wanting to know how I liked the Art Course. When she sensed my ill disguised disappointment that it was a lecture course, and not a hands on drawing class, she told me not to worry, but that she'd call and change the course for me.

When I showed up at the Art Institute the following week, I was ushered into a figure drawing class. Much to my surprise, it was a nude figure drawing class. I think I was, at age 12, probably the youngest to ever sit and draw female nudes.

Do you suppose that maybe, just maybe, that's why I admire looking at naked ladies to this day? Artistically speaking, of course!

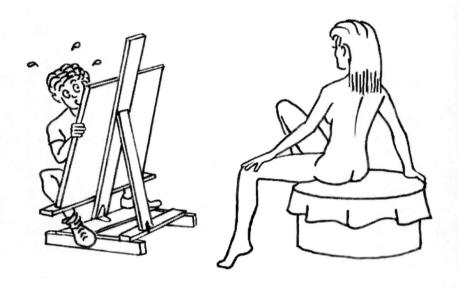

Then, again, while still appearing in this play, another form of Art Training was in store for me when we finally reached Los Angeles.

I remember a large park in the middle of Downtown LA that I would frequent during the day. It had a lake, paddle boats, and was quite an oasis in the heart of the city, much like Central Park is for residents of New York.

As I vaguely recall, the lake was fed by a concrete walled "canal", which had small bridges over which traffic and pedestrians passed. In this one particular spot, down beside the bridge footings at canal level, a legless Army veteran created incredibly beautiful sculptures in sand. People would always stop and watch, and more often than not, in recognition of his talent, would drop money down into a large "tub" below.

Apparently, he had been a fixture at this "stand" for some time. Sand was somehow or other brought in for him, and he, and his sand sculptures, were quite an attraction. We became good friends, since I'd stop by to watch him practically on a daily basis. He eventually invited me down to help him create these sculptures. I lugged water, sand, and learned to bulk up the subjects, smooth the surfaces, and developed a sculpter's "touch" with his help and guidance. Other than fooling around with colored clay as a child, it was my first hands on experience with a 3 dimensional art form. Although I still paint occasionally, I prefer sculpting to this day. But not in sand, thank you very much!

This is one of my sculptures currently in progress, titled "Capturing the Moon".

I work in clay, over a wire skeleton called an "armature", then make a mold, and cast in resin or bronze to make copies. The piece stands about 16" high, and represents an Indian maiden "bathing" in the rays of the full moon. As you can see, I'm still doing nude females.

It's a tough job...But someone has to do it! ☺

ACT 2

Scene 2

(Music up and under) "William Tell Overture" ......

(CUE NARRATION)

What better piece of music to use as an identifying theme for the early 40's? The segment from the William Tell Overture that heralded the approach of that heroic "Masked Rider"... thundering out of the West... on his great horse Silver.

O.K. Here we go. From this point on, I concentrate primarily on the "Golden Age of Radio".

To me, the Lone Ranger was a hallmark of Old Time Radio. Along with millions of other children my age, I was addicted to listening to the program. No matter what we kids were doing outdoors at the time, (playing ball, tag, or just plain hanging out), we all made a dash for home to tune in.

I mention this primarily to point out that, back then, I considered myself more of a "Fan" of radio programming, (and an avid listener of my favorite shows), than being a part of the medium as a "Performer". Go figure!

I suppose that stems from the fact that I was about 9 years old when I began working in earnest as a Child Actor in radio.

Having spent the previous 5 years doing print modeling and performing on the stage, it was just another assignment to me. But as luck would have it, (or by the grace of God), I was equipped to handle it. I had always been able to read well as a child, so sight reading for radio program auditions, and having learned about vocal inflections from my stage experience, made for an easy transition for me. I was spared having to "earn my spurs", and learn my craft, in what was to me a totally new work environment. Things just seemed to fall into place.

Don't ask me how I became known to radio Directors and Producers. "Known"...... in the sense that they would contact me to come in and read for any given part. I truly don't remember the mechanics of becoming a radio actor. All I can remember is that I started appearing on shows at that early age.

I think that it was Phil Lord, the Chicago radio actor who told my Mom about the "Ins and Outs" of the business. Much like she learned from other friends about who to contact regarding the plays I had been in. There were no "agents" as such for Radio. But I do know that an actor, to survive in the business, had to belong to either "Radio Registry" or "Lexington", or BOTH, if they wanted to be;

a) Known in the industry by people responsible for casting.
b) Easily contacted for auditions or bookings
c) Supplied with 3x5 index cards that had a small picture of the performer, a detailed list of one's credits and prior experience, other pertinent information such as "Age Range" (and when applicable), what "Dialects" they could handle. These "Cards" were then mailed or hand delivered to Directors, Ad Agency program producers, etc. Actually, once a performer gained lots of experience and reputation, they were used infrequently.

Being a client of Radio Registry or Lexington service served two basic functions. They acted as an answering service for all the NY area performers, and the index cards were a handy reference of available talent that Directors and Producers kept on file.

Below is the only "Registry" card that still exists among my souvenirs. Just like the photo composites for young models, these also had to be updated each year. Particularly when TV came along. (The face that appeared on the card was obviously more important then.) For radio work, one kept adding "Credits" that had been accumulated over time. I think this is the last card from my acting career that I bothered to have printed up. (circa 1950).

HARLAN STONE   RADIO REGISTRY
FL 9-6764

Type Work: Dramatic, Character actor, odd voice parts.

Dialects: Cockney, English, German, Spanish, (American dialects).

STAGE: (Harlan) in "Life With Father", "Lady in the Dark",
"Tomorrow the World", etc.

RADIO: Vicks Family of Five, Let's Pretend, Death Valley Days,
Dr. Christian, Road of Life, Right to Happiness, My True
Story, Henry Aldrich, Theater Guild, Maxie Rosenbloom Show,
Henry Morgan Show, Ethel Merman Show, Etc. Co-Star of the
"Archie Andrews Show" for the past six years in the char-
acter role of "Jughead".

SCREEN: Carnegie Hall, Whisting in Brooklyn, Army Signal Corps
films, etc.

TELEVISION: Henry Aldrich show, (Bing) in "Spring Green" on
Kraft T.V. theater. Guest Apppearance: Lanny Ross Show,
George Putnam show.

Voice Range: 15-25
Actual age: 20 (1951)
14 years an actor

Radio Registry would also publish and send out pictorial Talent "Directories". One paid a small fee to be included in these annual brochures that were sent to all the Agency Producers and Network Directors in the New York Area. Other major cities undoubtedly had similar publications. I know for a fact that L.A. did. I can only assume the same held true for cities like Detroit and Chicago, where other Network programming also originated.

As for the first N. Y. radio show I performed on when I returned from appearing in "Life With Father" ...... my mind is a trifle hazy. It probably started with a few appearances on "Let's Pretend", a very popular childrens program on Saturday mornings.

For the benefit of you "younger Pups" (those under 60) I had better reiterate what I said earlier. Unless you are a student (or fan) of Old Time Radio programs, or Show Biz in general, the names and careers of people I mention throughout this book may not ring a bell with you. But take it from me, they were all major players in the entertainment industry back in the '40's and '50's. Many (but not all) went on to substantial careers in TV and Motion Pictures. In the event you might wish to learn more about some of them, (and can access the Internet), here's the address of a Web Site that will give you in depth data about those early radio performers who went on to fame and fortune in TV and Films. Just log on to imdb.com and type in their names under the "People" catagory. I'll list some other OTR internet sites later in the back of the book.

As for reading material specifically geared towards the famous Radio shows of the 30's, 40's and early 50's. There are a number of books I could recommend. Some are truly scholarly works, listing Directors, Names of Characters, names of cast members, program outlines, etc. (See the suggested reading section at the end of this book.)   Most large public libraries probably have copies in the reference/reseach section.

But this book is simply about my memories of what it was

like being a young actor during radio's "Golden Age". It is not intended to go into great detail about the careers of the many performers I worked with over those years. I'll just mention some of their career highlights, and my personal recollections about them. Those other books go into far greater detail, and cover the full extent of their performing "credits" if that interests the reader.

Earlier, I told how the play "Life With Father" spawned a great many young actor's careers. Well, CBS's Saturday morning radio program "Let's Pretend" probably did far more in that regard. For those who do not recall that show, the cast was made up ENTIRELY of young actors. Some of the "regular" cast members actually grew up into young adulthood on that show. (Much like I did playing "Jughead" from age 14 to 23.

"Let's Pretend" was designed to appeal to young listeners, and featured dramatizations of ageless Fables and Fairy Tales. It put a whole host of kids to work over the 20 years the program was on the air. (1934-1954). However, since it was a Saturday morning program, (as was "Archie Andrews"), once I started playing Jughead, my "Let's Pretend" days were over.

I distinctly remember that program's Producer/Director, Nyla Mack. She was short. stocky, a husky voice, and had her hands full keeping a bunch of young kids in line. She was professional to the core, and didn't tolerate too much nonsense. One definitely learned to behave and pay attention... or you weren't hired again. Then too, the regulars on the show were all solid pros under her strict guidance, and it rubbed off on the newbies. I was impressed with the acting talents of many cast members that I grew up with. Among them, Donald Buka and Sybil Trent. And of course, Arthur Anderson, a perennial favorite of the OTR Convention crowd.

Donald Buka   Sybil Trent   Arthur Anderson

Donald Buka, in addition to being a Let's Pretend regular, was also busy working on other radio shows as well, and in the early years of live TV (1949-55), made numerous appearances on the dramatic shows originating out of New York (like Kraft Theatre and Philco Playhouse). Then, in the 60's, went to LA for notable appearances on many of the filmed TV dramas and Westerns being shot on the West Coast. Shows like "Perry Mason", "The Rebel", "Alfred Hitchcock Presents", "Lawman", "Gomer Pyle"…and the list goes on. He made his motion picture debut back in 1943 in the anti-war film "Watch on the Rhine". He followed that up with about 8 more film roles over the next 20 years. Donald is typical of the successful young actor, working in all mediums. That is of course, until Radio shows bit the dust. That narrowed the job opportunities down quite a bit, but TV programs eventually made up for that. With one caveat; Now the actor had to "look" the part, not just "sound" right.

Sybil Trent grew up on Let's Pretend since the age of 9. When she matured, Sybil also had featured roles on other radio shows such as the soap,"Stella Dallas". By the time "Let's Pretend" went off the air, she had already been married for three years, according to Arthur Anderson's book about that program.

106

Sybil also did a little TV work, but decided on a career behind the camera. She first became a talent agent, then a casting director for Young and Rubicam (one of New York's elite Advertising Agencies). Ocassionally I'd bump into her when I was hired to direct commercials for that agency in later years. She was as talented and charming as she was beautiful. Unfortunately, Sybil passed away about a year ago as of this writing.

Arthur Anderson is STILL doing "Lets Pretend". He can be seen at many of the OTR Conventions directing recreations of that show. However, back then, Arthur appeared on many other radio programs of that period, and did quite a bit of Theatre, TV and film work in the New York area as well. He appeared in the long running off broadway play, "The Fantastics", and the hit musical "1776", as well as several films. Arthur, like so many other radio performers, also found a niche doing TV commercials. He might be remembered as "Mr. Kuppeheimer" in the Kuppenheimer Men's Clothier's commercials for 7 years, and for about 29 years, he was the voice of the Leprechaun in the Lucky Charms breakfast cereal commercials.

How's that for a "Let's Pretenders" parlay? Sybil Trent cast people in commercials, Arthur appeared in them, and I wound up Directing them. Unfortunately, we all never connected on the same project.

I might as well spill the beans about some of the other Child Actors that were part of the scene back then. Although we would only work together occasionally, (depending on how many kids were needed on any given show), we certainly saw a lot of each other during auditions. We didn't socialize all that much outside the halls of NBC or CBS, but we'd gossip and tell jokes. I must confess, I don't remember what became of many of my childhood contemporaries, except for those who stayed in the "business" (in one form or another) and as adults, went on to have some success in TV and Motion Pictures . At this point, I might as well finish with those who appeared on "Let's Pretend' early in their lives.

Peter Fernandez was probably one of the best looking young men I ever met. Peter and I also had Child Modeling in common. We were both Powers models early in our careers, so we knew each other from way back. (Boy, when I reached the dating age I would have given anything to have his good looks instead of my freckled face and kinky red hair.) Peter went on to appear in many films and also did quite a bit of writing for films. I had a chance to see Peter at an Old Time Radio convention a few years back, and after 60+ years, he's still a handsome dog. And a super nice guy as well.

Jack Grimes was another classy guy and excellent actor. Short, (like a fairly tall and trim jockey), he was great fun to be around, had a wonderful personality, and although a little older than the rest of us young kids, treated us as equals. Jack was a sharp dresser. Always wore a tie and jacket. Interestingly enough, both he and Peter Fernandez went into business together following their performing days, and co-produced educational films. I should also point out that Jack originally played the part of "Archie Andrews" on WOR (before NBC took it over). More about that later.

Ronnie Liss was a good actor, worked a lot, but I don't think he was too well liked by the rest of us. I think one of the main reasons for that was his mother. A real no-nonsense lady who kept Ronnie on a tight leash and away from being contaminated by the rest of us "troublemakers". Ronnie worked quite a bit because he was good.  Very professional. But his Mom sure pushed him hard.

I should probably point out that some of the young actors that I mention in these pages were not necesasarily "regulars" on "Let's Pretend", but at least appeared on that program at one time or another during their early radio days. In many cases, I may not have worked with them on any other show, but at least knew them (and grew up with them) as part of the Child Actor fraternity.

Unfortunately, I couldn't find photos of some of them among my material, but I'll at least mention them. Michael Artist was a good kid, well liked, but was stuck wearing braces and had a slight lisp. Michael went to the same High School that I did. Kingsley Colton was another Child Model buddy, and a good friend. Kingsley quit performing when he matured, and following Military service, went with an Advertising Agency.

 Jack Ayers also attended High School with me. He left the performing end of the business, and eventually became a Brand Manager with the American Home Products company. As adults, my wife and I would ocassionally visit with Jack and his wife at their summer home on Long Island.

Billy (Bill) Lipton was a long time regular on Let's Pretend. And worked quite often on many other shows, particulary the soap operas. In the early to mid '40's, many of the "Let's Pretend" males, upon reaching draft age entered Military service. After discharge from the Navy, Bill took up where he left off as an actor. Unfortunately, illness interferred with Bill achieving a lengthy adult performing career.

Jackie Kelk   Walter Tetley   Cameron Andrews

Now here's an interesting trio. All three were known for "odd voiced" character parts on other programs. Jack Kelk was a fixture around CBS. He played "Homer" the sidekick to "Henry Aldrich" for many years.

Walter Tetley, one of the early "Let's Pretenders", ultimately had a long run playing the wize-cracking "Leroy", the nephew of "Throckmorton", on the immensely popular "The Great Gildersleeve".

Cameron Andrews worked on various programs, but he also played on "Archie Andrews". Ironically, he played "Jughead" alongside Jack Grimes when the show was first broadcast on WOR

Mutual. I never heard the program back then, and honest folks, I had no inkling as to what sort of voice he used to portray that character. I go on record and unequivocally state that I didn't copy his technique when I played the same role on NBC. (I'm not even sure if Cameron was in the running when NBC was casting the show)......For a change of pace, here's a bevy of lovely young ladies who were fixtures on the Radio scene back in those days.

Gerrianne Raphael   Florence Hallop   Marilyn Erskine

Gerrianne Raphael eventually went into the theatre and also did some TV work.

Florence Hallop had an extended career in television, appearing on a number of dramas and situation comedies. One of her better known roles was as a regular on TV's "Night Court".

Marilyn Erskine, following her NY Radio assignments in soaps and "Let's Pretend", went on to a substantial career on the west coast in the Theatre, Motion Pictures, and TV Sitcoms.

I should probably make this observation. As with most young children, the boys sort of hung out together. At our age it wasn't "cool" to hang around with Girls. One would get teased unmercifully, which I suppose was true in all walks of adolescent life.

Consequently, my recollections about any form of interaction with the younger female actresses is hazy at best. And naturally, the older girls, (fast becoming "Young Women") had their own clique, and little time for socializing with anyone not in their own age bracket. But that's not to say they weren't friendly and always pleasant to work with. Besides, I didn't attend the special schools in New York that many of these "child" actors attended, so my exposure to them was only when we worked together. That all changed when I went to High School. (But that part of the story comes later.) It's quite possible that I had an occasional adolescent crush on a few of them. (Or visa-versa I was later to discover).

Joan Patsy Flicker   Lorna Lynn   Betty Jane Tyler

These charming young ladies were closer to my age and we had a sort of mutual admiration society going. I seem to recall they all were on "Let's Pretend" around the same time I did the show, and we also saw each other often around the halls of NBC when working on other programs. And naturally, any child who could meet the exacting talent requirements that Nyla Mack imposed, and able to hone their acting skills on her show, often auditioned for parts on other Radio programs as well.

Joan Patsy Flicker had an extremely upbeat personality, was full of energy, and quick to turn on her smile.

Lorna Lynn's Mom must have spent hours doing her long blonde curls, and probably spent a small fortune on her frilly dresses. She always looked cute, prim and very "ladylike".

But of the three, I seem to recall once having a "Date" with Betty Jane. It probably was nothing more than having a soda together in the local coffee shop on the ground floor of NBC. Betty was a few years older than I was, and she may well have done the inviting. I was just a shy young teenager. Obviously, even at that tender age, I was attracted to "older" women. Betty Jane was very warm hearted and comfortable to be around.

Despite the heavy competition among the many child actors that were in the business back then, I don't recall too many petty jealousies or resentment for those who got lucky and had steady work. Other than the programs that featured young actors on a regular basis, the parts for children on night time dramas and daytime soaps were not all that plentiful. I suppose some kids had problems handling rejection if they lost an audition, but if that was the case, I blame the parents for pushing them too hard. I'm sure some got discouraged early on and dropped out, but there were always newcomers to take up the slack. And "Let's Pretend" was always on the lookout for talented newcomers in addition to the show's firmly entrenched regular cast members.

 Speaking of "regulars", Bill Adams was a fixture on "Pretend" for many years. He portrayed the kindly narrator, "Uncle Bill". As evidenced by the "WABC" microphone in the photo, he was a popular and busy performer on the other Networks as well. I often worked with him over at NBC.

You will undoubtedly recall my going into detail about this "Life With Father graduate. Among his many Radio credits, my good buddy Ben Cooper was also a member of the "Let's Pretend" cast before heading westward for his highly successful TV and film career.

Skippy Homeier, another friend of mine, also achieved stardom in TV and motion pictures following his NY theatre and radio days. Skip had the starring role in the Broadway production of "Tomorrow the World", and also starred in the film adaptation. Skip appeared in well over 110 TV shows and films, including the title role in the "Dan Raven" Police series. It would take two pages just to list all his credits. Skip tells great stories (not for publication) about how both he and Ben Cooper drove out west together to seek more fame and fortune in "Tinsel Town" and of the bachelor pad they shared for awhile. In later years,(just as I did with Ben Cooper), I had the great pleasure to work with Skip a few times when I became a director of TV commercials.

Larry Robinson was also a "Life With Father" graduate, in addition to earning his stripes on "Let's Pretend", Larry also played opposite Gertrude Berg (as her son "Sammy") in the successful radio and TV series, "The Goldbergs".

How about this little cutie. She grew up to be a successful actress, easily making the transition to TV and Films. This photo was taken when, as youngsters, we both appeared on Broadway in the play titled "This Rock". The name of this charming young lady; Joyce Van Patten.

114

You got it! The younger sister of another neat guy, Dick Van Patten. Dick had a formidable Radio and TV career. After outgrowing "Let's Pretend" a major TV role came his way. He played "Nels" on the popular TV show "I Remember Mama". And most everyone (regardless of age) will remember Dick's portrayal of the  father on the long running TV sitcom "Eight is Enough". At this writing, Dick is just finishing up a nationwide tour with Frank Gorshin in their revival of Neil Simon's "The Sunshine Boys".

 No stranger to Dick Van Patten, and a close friend and co-worker of mine for many years, was the very talented actress Rosemary Rice. Rosemary played Dick's older sister "Katrin' in "I Remember Mama", and for many years played "Betty" on our "Archie Andrews" radio show. As a matter of fact, Rosemary was still doing the "Archie" radio show in the early '50's while appearing on TV in "Mama". I'll have much more to say about Rosemary later.

Talk about friends and co-workers; this character was a good friend to both Rosemary and me. After he was cast as the first "Archie" during it's run on NBC, Charlie Mullen's "Let's Pretend" days came to a screeching halt due to the Saturday morning time conflict . Regardless of any scheduling conflict, Nyla Mack demanded a certain  degree of loyalty. According to Arthur Anderson's book, there was quite a bit of competition between CBS and NBC.

Nyla, as head of Children's programming for CBS, was locked in a battle with Madge Tucker, her counterpart at NBC. Both Networks were trying to capture the largest share of listening audience, regardless of time of day. The more popular and successful the program, the greater the chance to attract a sponsor. Making money for the Network was the name of the game, and advertising dollars was the lifeblood that sustained them. Neither Nyla nor Madge was thrilled if any of their "Brood" was unavailable when they wanted to use them, particularly if it was discovered that the kid was working for the competition that day. After reading Arthur's book, I was left with the impression that Nyla Mack was a bit of a martinet. She ruled with an iron hand. If a young performer (of any age) demonstrated loyalty, (as well as affection), and met her criteria for availability and professional acting standards, they were on the "A" list of talent for her to draw on. But it seems one would fall rapidly from grace if these conditions were not met.

Fortunately, I was not affected by this tug of war between the two networks, and their respective heads of Children's programming. Once I started performing on "Archie", it was a non-issue because of the time conflicts. To close the subject of "Let's Pretend", I'll mention two more acting friends that appeared on that program, and who I also worked with on the stage.

Joan Shepard was a fine little actress, and very bright. Having been born in England, she worked hard to tone down her British accent. Joan and I were in the nationwide tour of the hit play "Tomorrow the World". Joan had the female child lead, and was a no nonsense performer.

In that same production was another fellow stage actor named Mack Twombley. Aside from a little radio work, I have no idea what ever happened to him. But that was often the case with child actors. Often, they were in the business because their parents wanted them to be. When they matured, or when they weren't getting the breaks, and working enough, they were obligated to find other ways to earn a living.

O.K. That does it as far as the people I knew and worked with who were "Let's Pretend" graduates. By my count, I mentioned about 30 of them. In Arthur Anderson's book, he either mentions (or lists) a total of 175 actors or actresses who appeared on the show over the many years it was broadcast. Wow! Young performers must have been a glut on the market. But like I just mentioned above, I think the attrition rate must have been fairly extensive. Only the best (and/or luckiest) survived as performers, while others found work in the creative and production end of the industry.

In all likelihood, my second big break in radio as a 9 year old was probably getting a running part on the show "The Nichols Family of Five", playing the youngest child in the family. It starred a very popular radio actor of that period, Matt Crowley, (a super nice man). I vaguely recall the original title was changed to "The Vicks Family of Five", after Vicks picked up the sponsorship of the program. (Money talks, right?) It was originally a sustaining program, with very modest talent fees. And it's quite possible that I had to leave the show before it became sponsored, because I was hired to appear in another play. My folks always made those decisions, and it was simply a matter of which job opportunity paid the most money. During this period, I was still involved with appearances in other Stage Productions, consequently, I was in and out of the New York job market as a Radio performer.

But I have distinct recollections of working on that show as a child, primarily because the cast was so friendly, and very helpful with teaching me some of the tricks of the trade connected with radio acting. Matt Crowley in particular. He took the time to teach me some of the fundamentals, like the proper way to "mark" a script so my lines of dialogue were readily identified on the page, thus preventing me from losing my place. Also, that it was better to remove the staple holding the pages of the script together, so that when it was time to go to the next page, one could quietly slide the finished page behind the others at the back of the script. In this case, being right handed, I held the entire script in my left hand, and while reading, I isolated the top page with the fingers of my right hand, and slipped it behind the others at the appropriate time. It took a little practice, but it was the best way to prevent the sound of rustling paper when working close to the microphone.

I also learned proper microphone etiquette from Matt. Being short, (age 9) it was necessary for me to stand on a little rug covered platform to get close to the mike for my lines. These "boxes" usually were standard equipment in the studios. (Readily available whenever small children were performing on any given program). The rug covering on top helped deaden the hollow sound when a kid stepped up on it. But it was important to also learn how to sway

118

your body off to one side after delivering your line, so that a grown actor, using the same side of the mike, could get a word in edge-wise. (Oh Gosh! Another pun!)

One other very clear memory from working on that show was an incident that happened when the cast was sitting around the rehearsal table doing a first "read through" of the script. This usually was the first step before going "on mike" to rehearse, giving the cast a chance to familiarize themselves with the dia-logue, and the director a chance to get a rough timing and "feel" for the pacing of any given scene.

In one of the early episodes, I had a line referring to my having been outdoors in the cold. I was supposed to say, *"And I almost caught pneumonia"*. (Sure! Easy for you to say). Although I was only nine years old I was able to read fairly well, but that didn't prevent me from having a problem pronouncing difficult and unfamiliar words. When I got to that line, I pronounced the ailment as "PEE-NOME-E-AH", at which point, the entire cast cracked up. Between chuckles, Matt, who was sitting next to me, explained how the word was pronounced, but the Director, still smiling said. *"No, Harlan, keep saying it the same way. That's funny. That's the way a young kid would pronounce it anyway"*.

I probably could easily have been embarrassed by my goof, but the good natured laughter from the rest of the cast, and the director's approval, taught me that I enjoyed making people laugh. Later on in life, playing "Jughead" provided lots of opportunities to do just that.

Speaking of later on in life, let's fast forward briefly. When I became a TV Director, It was a real treat for me to able to hire

people that I had once worked with in radio when I was a youngster. Generally, I sought out those performers who had been so
kind to me back then. Matt Crowley was definitely one of them.

As far as other programs that I worked on in the early 40's, I
remember occasional appearances on most of the soaps of the day,
such as "My true Story", "Road of Life", "Right to Happiness",
,"Portia Faces Life", etc.

I don't recall if any of them were "running parts" of any
duration...... Just that I worked those shows. Unlike my Modeling
or Theatre experiences, my folks did not maintain a scrapbook (or
Journal) that kept track of my radio performances. I only
remember all those shows because my Radio Registry card
indicates that these programs were my more "notable" radio
performance "credits" over those years.

Obviously, the more shows that one did, the more that
Directors were aware of one's talent and experience, and the more
likely one was called upon to audition for other roles. In many
cases, when a Director became familiar with an actor's work, you
would often be spared the auditioning process and simply called
and booked for a particular part.

But auditions were quite common. You soon learned to take it
in stride that some other actor might win the part. A"Many are
called...few (only one) are chosen" sort of thing. But that was the
way things worked. Win some, lose some. As long as you won
more than you lost, one could have a viable career in the business.

Besides, it wasn't incumbent on me to desperately seek work
to earn a living. Unlike mature actors, I didn't have to support

myself, much less a family. By that point in time, my Father, the "Iceman" found gainful employment in other endeavors, so the money I earned was frosting on the cake. Consequently, I had no pressure on me to compete for the "Brass Ring" on a daily basis.

That made working in the business fun. Besides, when one went for auditions, you got to meet and pal around with other kids the same age, and it was sort of a young actors "Club". Usually the same ones would show up, and you could develop friendships and associations, despite the competition. It was the "Stage Mothers" who sometimes accompanied their "Child Wonders" that usually were a pain in the butt. Thankfully, my Mom let me go in the City on my own from about age 10 on. (It was a lot safer to ride the NY subways back then.) Besides, I was incredibly erudite and sophisticated at a tender age. Hah! But growing up in Show Business as I did, one couldn't help but become "street smart" and aware of one's surroundings. Also, it helped me obtain a degree of maturity far beyond that of kids who had more normal childhood backgrounds.

During those early years, some of the other shows I did may ring a bell to many who lived through that period. They were quite popular and memorable. Such as "Dr. Christian", "Big Town", "Death Valley Days", to name a few. As I mentioned earlier, in almost all instances they were not necessarily starring roles or parts that lasted over many episodes. That was particularly true of the anthology type of show that presented a new story every week.

Generally, as a child actor, one was called on to perform in a supporting role, or small bit parts, depending on the story line. It really didn't matter, as long as the work was relatively steady. Basically, when one performed on a "sustaining" radio program,

121

(no commercial sponsor), one received a set fee. A commercially sponsored Network prime time program paid much more. Usually supporting actors were paid the same, regardless of the size of the part. The minimum pay scale was set by the radio performers union, known back then as AFRA (American Federation of Radio Artists). Of course, the Stars of a show could negotiate higher fees.

As a young adult, I performed on quite a few other Radio Programs in my late teens and early 20s. These were just some that I did before I quit performing on the Stage at age 13. That's when I concentrated on Radio Acting full time. (The Archie Andrews Show had a great deal to do with that decision, but that's a whole 'nuther story in the next "Scene".)

For those of you OTR Radio buffs who might be disappointed that I can't go into more detail with recollections about those early years,......please cut me some slack. Heck, I was only a kid, and what do kids know? (And no, you can't get your money back). ☺ But I promise...... my memory improves greatly from age 14 on, so be patient.

But I do remember appearing on "Dr. Christian" a few times.

I recall that program's star, Jean Hersholt as being a very kind and friendly older man, much like the character he played. "Type Casting" of the highest order. Mr. Hersholt had an incredibly diverse career in the Entertainment industry. He was born in Europe of Danish parents (who were also performers). He did a few silent films in Europe before coming to the United States in 1915. Much like Lillian Gish, he had an incredible silent film career, appearing in about 60 of them between 1906-1927. He made the difficult transition to the "talkies" after having worked on toning down his accent, which of course was not an issue when he worked in all those Silent Films. He appeared in about 70 more motion pictures once talkies came on the scene, but I don't think there is any question that his most memorable role in film was as "Dr. Christian". He made 6 movies playing that lovable character between 1939/41. But he has to have a special niche among Old Time Radio fans for also playing "Dr. Christian" on radio for about 17 years.

For those readers who might not remember all the awards they give out each year during the annual Academy Awards telecast, one of the more notable "Oscars" is presented to the individual who has made significant humanitarian contributions to the Motion Picture Industry and society in general. That Oscar is justifiably named in his honor, and called, "The Jean Hersholt Humanitarian Award". He was much beloved by all in Show Business, not only for his consumate skill as an actor, but for the many charitable causes that he supported, and to which he dedicated so much of his time, energy and money.

My other recollection of Mr. Hersholt is that he had an incredible mane of hair. I was glad to see that I was not the only one who had unmanageable kinky curls. The preceeding photo of him was taken about the time I appeared on his program. His hair was grey by then, and he was probably in his late fifties.

One other neat tid-bit of information about Jean Hersholt. He is the uncle of film and TV actor Leslie Nielson, who stars in the series of recent detective film spoofs, the "Naked Gun" .

Looking back on my acting years in the theater and radio, I suppose my only regret was that I was too young to appreciate the history and background of people that were so famous long before I was born. I never realized they were such big stars back then. But that was primarily due to the fact that they didn't go around acting like celebrities with huge egos. (Unlike some of the later day TV and Film actors who believe all their press clippings and refuse to recognize the fact that they are mere mortals like the rest of us.) With those "bozo's", a certain arrogance sets in, and they become truly unbearable.

But such was not the case with ANY of the truly wonderful performers I worked with over my years in the theatre and radio. (Except for maybe Gertrude Lawrence). Ah! but some of the actors/actresses that I encountered later on during my 25 years in TV left me with far less positive memories.

But I definitely have many fond memories about Rosemary DeCamp. Rosemary played Dr. Christian's nurse, "Judy", for the long run on that same program. A truly lovely, and very attractive lady. She was very nice to me, and treated me as a contemporary, not some "wet behinds the ears" kid. I worked on a few other radio programs with her, and she was definitely a favorite of mine.

Back then, Rosemary was a very popular actress in radio, and her career later blossomed with many appearances in motion pictures and TV. Ultimately, she did about 23 films, and over 37 TV shows, notably, running parts on "Petticoat Junction", "That Girl" , The "Bob Cummings Show", etc. She also guest starred on TV series such as " The Partdrige Family", "Beverly Hillbillys", "Rockford Files","Love Boat", " St. Elsewhere", etc.

Have you noticed that during Motion Picture and TV Awards acceptance speaches, one often hears the performer give thanks to their agent for finding parts for them to play. In my opinion, Rosemary DeCamp's agent should have gotton down on his knees every night to give thanks that he had such a talented, well liked, and well respected performer to represent.

When I moved to Sedona, Arizona in the early '90s, I discovered that Rosemary DeCamp had been raised in a nearby Copper Mining town called Jerome. I believe her father had been the Jerome mine Forman or Manager. I was saddened to hear that she passed away recently. If you'd like to learn more about this multi talented actress, she wrote a memoir titled "Stories from Hollywood" that was published in 1991 as an audio book.

Another favorite of mine was Jan Miner. I worked with her more than a few times, and fell more and more in love with her on each occasion. I'm serious. You can call it puppy love if you want. or, infatuation, but she sure stirred something in my adolecent breast. Now in my old age, I can identify it. It was lust . The pre-teen version I suppose.

Jan usually wore high heels, (had great legs), a tight white buttoned-down-the-front blouse that she filled out admirably, and a form fitting skirt. Top that off with her charming personality and warmth, and I was definitely smitten. There certainly were times in my life that I yearned to be older and in her league. She was a very classy lady. And a very hard working and busy radio actress. She had a number of running parts on the soaps of the day, and was a front runner when directors were casting other programs. When TV came along, she easily made the transition to that medium, particularly in the early days of live dramatic shows. She was almost a fixture on "Robert Montgomery Presents", and played many parts on that program throughout the early '50s. She appeared in a few films, but the bulk of her credits were in New York Television, with appearances on "Naked City", the daytime TV soap "The Nurses", "Alcoa Presents", "The Defenders", "Law & Order", Etc.

Some of you will recall that she went on to TV Advertising fame and fortune, and for years, played "Marge the Manicurist", (who recommended soaking in Palmolive Dishwashing Detergent). Usually in a "close up", so one couldn't see her other formidable charms. (Gee, I better get off this kick so I can concentrate on writing the rest of this book). Jan did those commercials for ALMOST 20 YEARS! I was thrilled for her. They had to have provided her with a comfortable living. I can almost bet that in the final year that those spots ran on National TV, her talent fees for doing them eclipsed the total amount of money she earned in all her years as a radio actress in those early days.

Unfortunately, I never had the opportunity to work with Jan when I began directing. But if I had, I definitely would have told her about the major crush I had on her when I was a young kid.

Perhaps now would be as good a time as any to familiarize the reader with the typical radio studio set up and work environment. The only difference... the size of the studio. The really large studios were designed to specifically accomodate studio audiences, with most of the space set aside for seating. But when you got right down to it, the actual area used by the performers was pretty standard, and didn't take up too much room unless a studio orchestra was involved. (But then, a larger stage would be used.)

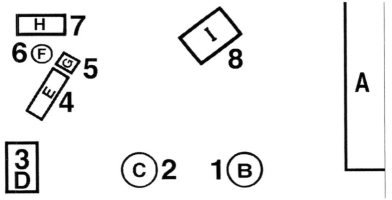

The numbers represent the position of studio microphones. (#5 no mike. Just a direct wire patch into control room).
A: Control room (director ,engineer, writer, etc).
B & C: Actors: Up to eight performers could be on just 2 mikes at the same time. Two to each side of a mike.
D: Sound proof Filter booth for "telephone" voice effect.
E: SFX (sound effects) work surface for hand held objects (Utensils, phone,dishes, crunching snow, horse hoofs. etc.)
F: Portable wood flooring for footsteps, chair scrapes. etc.
G:Turntable for recorded SFX.
H: Portable door (or window sash).
I: Organ and organist for musical intro and bridges.
NOTE: Diagram not to scale.

The larger studios that held audiences usually had a raised stage, (for better audience viewing) and some even had inclined floors, with aisle steps leading to the seat rows that went as high as the next floor above. But the actual working area for performers and sound effects was not much bigger than those found in smaller studios. Think of the smaller ones as just fairly large rooms. Many of the soaps and dramatic shows were broadcast from them.

This NBC studio is really a hybrid; quite a bit larger than the standard size "smaller studio", and with a unique raised stage platform. The smaller studios all had level floors. The bare area in the foreground was used to put folding chairs to accomodate a small studio audience. The larger studios had fixed plush seating for audience comfort. Note the control room (far rear window) . The "nearer" window was what we called the "Client's Booth", used infrequently by sponsors, agency people, network brass or guests. Also note the unusual rear and side walls, as well as the ceiling treatment. These were sound baffles, designed to control room echo and room tone, so if one had to shout, it wouldn't sound like it was coming from a cave. As you can see from the single microphone, there would be ample room to put 4 people around it.

I think I should now say something about the unsung heros of radio broadcasting, the audio engineers. Take a close look at the opposite photo again. See the little grey rectangle near the floor underneath the control room window. That's the microphone patch panel. All those microphone placements that I showed in the earlier diagram had to be strung along the floor (out of the way so people wouldn't be tripping over them) then connected to jacks in this patch panel. This was done prior to each show. Inside the control room, each mike was then controlled by a seperate knob or "pot'. The engineer had a series of meters and knobs on his large control panel so that he could set (and maintain) proper audio levels for each microphone during the course of the program. Obviously, he was kept pretty busy. But during rehearsals, he could get familiar with what was required, and could pre-set his levels as a general rule. But he still " rode" the main mixed output control, to make sure acceptable broadcast levels (volume) was maintained, and was balanced between the different sources of sounds, such as music and sound effects. After all, the dialogue had to be heard and couldn't be drowned out by those other elements. That's why I consider engineers "artists", who played their console knobs with great skill. They were a very important part of all radio broadcasts.

When I did the Archie show, we used this exact studio shown here for a brief period in late 1951. During the Korean War, I was called to active duty in the U.S. Air Force. My outfit was temporarily stationed in New Hampshire. I was able to get weekend passes and travel back to NY to still play "Jughead" but couldn't make it in time for the 10:30 AM Saturday morning live broadcast. I'm pleased to report that NBC, the cast and director, all made major consessions in my behalf. We recorded the program on Saturday evenings in this studio, for playback on the following Saturday morning in the regular time slot. That is, until my unit had to ship out to Newfoundland. We didn't need a larger studio because our Saturday night schedule pretty much ruled out children (our main fan base) being able to attend the recording session. Then too, the larger studio we normally used on Saturday mornings may have been booked for something else at night.

Now, getting back to my early career. During the 40's, in addition to my theatre work and appearing on various radio shows, I was also cast in two motion pictures that were being shot in New York, and also made a few screen tests for others. I came close to getting the lead in a west coast film titled the "Red Pony", but someone else got the final nod. As for the two films shot in NY, they certainly were not major roles by any means, and in the final analysis, most of my scenes ended up on the infamous "cutting room floor". When doing a movie, one never knew how many (or how much) of one's scenes would remain in the final cut.

The first film starred Red Skelton, in one of his famous "Whistling" movies. This one titled "Whistling in Brooklyn", and my role, along with some other kids, were as fans of the Brooklyn Dodgers who were attending a game at the the old Ebbets Field ballpark with Red. Not much survived the final edit. But it was fun getting to meet and work with that great comedian. The other Film was a high brow musical called "Carnegie Hall". I had some scenes as a young fan of the great Cellist of that period, Gregor Piatirgorsky. Again, not much survived. No matter... it paid well.

130

I suppose this film work also counted. During the war years, the Army Signal Corps shot documentaries at their studios directly across the river from Manhatten in an area called Long Island City. I did a few films for them, in nameless kid parts.

I guess you'll agree with me when I say I had a most unusual and unique childhood. But I didn't realize it back then. I sort of took things for granted. Maybe a bit too blasé about my lifestyle. I still did things other kids my age did… when I wasn't working.

I played sandlot baseball and football around my hometown, hung out with my neighborhood buddies, and even had the occasional fistfight with a few "bullies". I was sometimes picked on by a few of my peers who thought I was either stuck-up, too well mannered, a "teachers pet", or had to dress too "neatly". (My Folks never knew when I might have to be called out of school to go for a Modeling job or Audition, so I couldn't wear normal school yard attire.)

I was able to hold my own in those instances, and usually became good friends with the adversaries afterwards. Although my "celebrity" status provided me with some wonderful experiences, there were occasional downsides. Enough so, that I wouldn't wish a career in Show Business on my own Children. Much to my daughter's chagrin. And I think she still harbors a little resentment over it. However, it certainly worked out well for me down the road. But I think I was lucky. As they say…" Timing is everything in life". That's particularly true in Show Business.

In case there are some readers who might be mildly interested in what sort of schooling working Child Actors obtained, I'll touch on it briefly.

In the N.Y. area, there were primarily three schools that catered to us stage brats. The largest, and most notable, was called PCS (Professional Childrens' School). The curriculum was so set up that the kids could get out of class at any time of the school day, to either go for an audition, appear in a radio program, or go to a Broadway theatre for a Wednesday matinee. The school understood the need for flexible attendance, and arranged for make-up exams, or review of any lesson material that was missed. I did not attend PCS. My Mom had connections elsewhere.

It seems that as a young girl growing up in Whitestone, (a small community on Long Island), she attended St. Luke's Parochial school. Not because she only lived a block away, (and was Catholic), but because her father was the Church sextant and school janitor. So it was ordained (and practically mandated) that I also go there when I reached grade school age. She was in solid with all the nuns, and in particular with the Mother Superior that had taught her as a child. With her clout and connections, I was given special consideration, and allowed absences for modeling and show business activities. As a matter of fact, I was "adopted" by many of the Nun's, who enjoyed my "celebrity" status. At times, I felt like the school mascot. (No wonder some of other kids picked on me.)

Even when I went out of town for an acting assignment, classwork was sent to me and I was home schooled to some extent. And when in Chicago with "Life With Father", I was able to attend the local Catholic school near the hotel, since we were there for such a long time. (The NY Nun Connections got me in.)

Later on, during the run of "Tomorrow the World" , Elissa Landi's husband, Curtis Thomas, travelled with us. He was an educator, and schooled all 6 kids in the cast of that play. And of course, my Mother and her Nun connections saw that I was promoted to the next grade in the local school upon my return home.

Another educational option for performing children was attending "The Burton School for Professional Children". I really didn't know much about it at the time, but it sure is a small world. When I went to college years later, one of my classmates was an aspiring actress named Mimi Cuzzens, who achived success in Show Biz after graduating, (and who I was able to use in a few things when I became a director). Mimi is still going strong as an actress. But the point of the story is that we just recently got back in touch after 20 years, and she now informs me that her mother ran the aformentioned Burton School. It seems Rita Moreno was one of the star pupils.

The third School in NYC attended primarily by Child Performers was The Lodge School. Much smaller than PCS, but every bit as flexible regarding attendance. I went there after graduating from Grade school, and only spent my first two years of High School there, trying to do as little school work as possible. Some of the other "notable" young performers that also attended that school were the singing "DeMarco Sisters" (who appeared on Fred Allen's Program) and a wannabe comedian (of the Borsht Belt school), named Bobby Ramsen..

But I wanted to play organized High School football, so my folks arranged a transfer to a private school named McBurney for my final two years of High School. I attended The Lodge School and McBurney during the first four years that the" Archie" Show was on the air.

Although McBurney was not necessarily geared for kids in Show Business, concessions were easily obtained. Unfortunately, it was an all boy's school, so I missed out on a co-ed atmosphere. (At that age, I was as interested in girls every bit as much as being a "Jock" and playing football.) And since it was in NYC, I had to lose sleep and get up way too early to make the hour trip into town. (At least I could do a little studying on the train.) Ha! Very little!

There were a few other male child actors who also went to McBurney, (located on 63rd street across from Central Park West). Jack Ayers and Michael Artist, who I mentioned earlier, also went there. Then too, a kid who was a few years behind me, attained recognition in later years as a very controversial "shock jock" radio talk show host... Morton Downey Jr.

One of the really neat things about going there was the fact that they allowed me to take the Art courses they offered as a Major, and get credit for them that way. Normally, they were an elective, with only minor credits. It sure helped pick up my grade average. One of my Art class mates was a guy named Jacques LaTour, who went on to a notable career as an Art Director for a major NY Ad Agency. Bless him! In later years Jacques hired me as a Director for some of the TV ads he was responsible for.

But for the most part, I hung out with all the guys from the football team. In nice weather, we generally ate lunch together, sitting on benches in Central Park, which was a half block away. It at least assured me of palling around with normal kids my age.

Did I say "normal"? Well ...at least most of them were...

And then there was Billy Lewis!!!

Bill was one of the notable exceptions to the rule. We met on the Football team, and became really good friends. (We've stayed that way for well over 50 years.)

BILLY   ME

Note the fact that we didn't have nose guards back then. So what if a few blows to my nose eliminated my "Cute Kid" status, and made it a little bigger than before. It gave it character, as the expression goes.

Bill went from High School into the Army during the Korean War. Upon discharge, he joined the NYC Police Department, eventually becoming a Gold Shield detective. But like most policemen back then, he needed to "moonlight" in some sort of part-time job to support his growing family.

Bill came to see me one day during the years when I was a TV Director, and wanted to know if he could "moonlight" as an actor in commercials and pick up a few bucks that way. Since he

135

was always a "ham" and a cut-up during High School, I figured he had enough "moxie" to at least take a stab at working in TV commercials. If nothing else, at least as an "extra" on occasion. I showed him how to get composite photographs made, and helped him join the performers union, by throwing a few jobs his way.

BILL LOUIS

I gave him nothing of major consequence to do, because I wasn't sure he could handle any serious acting, and I wasn't about to compromise my professional standards in case he was lousy.

I think the first assignment I gave him, just so he could join the Union, was as an "extra" in the background of an auto repair shop setting. All he had to do was lie under a car with just his legs showing. I felt reasonably sure he couldn't screw that up.

To make a long story short, after a few shaky and slightly nervous starts, he took to performing in commercials like he'd been doing it all his life. He ultimately became so successful, that he quit the NY Police force after 16 years, because that full-time day job interfered with all his acting assignments. I take no credit for that. He did it on his own. All he needed was to have a door or two opened at the start.

And he's still at it, appearing in a lot of "regional" theatre productions. (Although he's lost his boyish good looks.)

There were only two reasons for me to digress from my story and tell you about my good buddy Billy. First and foremost, we hung out together during my teenage acting years. He attended performances of the Archie Andrews show fairly regularly. (We usually found mischief to get into following the Saturday broadcasts). I had some semblance of a normal teenage life with guys like Bill as my friend, and used this story to illustrate that point.

The second reason is probably the most significant. By mentioning him in this book, he'll probably tell a few thousand people to go out and buy a copy.

Like I said…He's a big ham, and either wants to see his name up in lights, or barring that, in the pages of a book. What's not to love about the guy?

Act 2

Scene 3

(Music up and under) "My Comic Valentine"

(CUE NARRATION)

I was called in to audition for the part of "Jughead" on the "Archie Andrews Show" back in 1944, immediately after NBC obtained the Broadcast Rights from John Goldwater and Louis Silberkleit, co-founders of Archie Comic Publications.

The "Archie" Characters first appeared as a separate feature in an earlier comic book published under the name "Pep Comics" in late 1941, (which was also published by these same gentlemen). However, the company back then was known as MLJ Magazines, and had its start in 1939. Due to the early success and popularity of "Archie" and his gang, the Characters were spun off into their own exclusive comic book identity (Archie Comics), with the first edition published in late 1942. It became, and remains to this day, a very popular comic book among the 7 to 14 year old age set. The success of the "Archie" comic book brought about a name change for the Publishing firm in 1946… to that of Archie Comic Publications.

The "Archie" Comic Characters are celebrating their 60th

Year Anniversary in 2002. And they are still "Teenagers" in Riversdale High School. Their appeal as Comic Book Characters for younger readers has never wavered, amd is probably due to its wholesome story lines, and cast of endearing characters, who engage in all sorts of typical Teenage activities and situations with a humorous twist.

In all liklihood, the parents of young children today probably read the Archie Comic Book, as did their grandparents before them. It's "squeaky clean" and non-controversial entertainment value is an oasis in todays plethora of Sex, violence and mayhem. Definitely not "R" or "X" rated, and for that reason alone, is welcomed into family homes all across America.

It pleased me to learn, when I was researching a few things for this book, that the two gentlemen currently running Archie Comic Publications, are the sons of the original founders. It's sure nice to know that some things still endure in this fast changing world. Archie Comics is the only family-owned and independent comic book publisher in the industry.

My thanks to Michael Silberkleit and Richard Goldwater, the current Head Honcho's at Archie Comics, for their assistance when I needed my memory refreshed. And what I found to be even more gratifying, Michael tells me that both he and Richard often talk about the "old days" when the "Archie Andrews" program was on radio, and fondly remember (as young children) being brought into the studio by their fathers to watch some of the broadcasts. And I believe that these two gentlemen are in their 60's...DO I FEEL OLD, OR WHAT!

I also believe that the popularity and success of "Archie

Andrews" on radio (over such a long period of time) probably contributed to the success of the Archie Comics due to the national exposure of the characters on Network radio, and the way the program was written to appeal to the target audience, Americas' 7 to 14 year olds.

As I recall, the NBC general audition for "teenagers" to play the main Characters was a "Cattle Call". (The term we used to refer to certain kinds of auditions back then) Simply stated, any and all teenage child actors, that had a modicum of radio experience and demonstrated some semblance of talent, were scheduled to read for the part. They showed up in droves, hence the term "Cattle Call".

The Director in charge of the auditions was Anton (Tony) Leader. The administrative assistants in the casting department would stagger the audition "call times", probably 10 minutes apart, so the area outside Studio 3B wouldn't get too clogged with the hopeful and aspiring candidates for the four "juicy" parts that were up for grabs, "Archie" ,"Jughead", "Betty" and "Veronica".

In extensive casting sessions like that, it was usually a weeding out process. Everyone scheduled would get a chance to look the audition script over before going into the studio, (to familiarize themselves with the dialogue), then be called in one at a time to read "on mike" for the Director, (and other interested parties), who were sitting in the control room behind the big sound proof plate glass window.

I recall when it was my turn, Tony Leader, (who I had worked for prior to this audition), pressed his "Talk Back" button as I entered the studio and said over the speaker *"Hello, Harlan. How're you doing?"* I'd of course wave at him, and reply into the microphone, *"Fine, Mr. Leader"*.

He then asked if I was familiar with the Archie Andrews Comic Book characters, and I indicated that I was. He then said, *"What I'd like you to do for me is to read the part the way you think "Jughead" would sound. You know what he looks like. How do you think he'd sound? The only thing I ask is that you don't make him sound like "Homer" on the "Henry Aldrich" show, O.K.?."* I nodded I understood, and replied *"Yes Sir"*. He then said, "Any questions?" I responded *"No sir!"* He said " *Great, let's go. On my cue"*. He turned to say something to some other people sitting behind him in the glass encased Control Room, turned back to face me standing in front of the mike, then "threw" me the hand cue to start. (An index finger pointed in my direction).

I honestly don't remember who read opposite me during the audition. I don't think they were trying to cast both parts simultaneously. That can get too confusing. At any rate, after doing a brief scene, Tony Leader looked up from writing some notes, turned to say something else to the people behind him, then "keyed" his talk-back mike and said, *"Thanks, Harlan, we'll let you know"*. The standard line... after almost all "General" auditions.

When I left the studio, there was still a bunch of kids waiting to read for the part. The routine of auditioning went on for quite a while. All us "cattle" were given their chance to moo a bit. There were no young ladies among the "hopefuls", so it was obvious that they were being auditioned separately at some other time.

The "Kids" that were called that day, (or for any other major audition), were always a study in contrasts. The older boys, (age 18 and up who could "play" younger) were usually "strictly business" ...friendly, but highly competitive. After all, it was their bread & butter. For many of those older kids, (at that stage in their lives) performing was their principal means of economic survival if they no longer lived at home with their parents. Besides, there wasn't all that much work to go around in the Teenage range, so getting a job was serious business to them.

However, many of the younger kids (early teens) would often treat these casting sessions as a lark, which simply gave them opportunities to see childhood acting buddies that they worked with over the years, and kid around with each other while waiting to be called. Typical teenage interaction, but not too boisterous there in the Hallowed Halls of NBC. Then too, if you took these "Job Hunting" sessions too seriously, and didn't get the part, the rejection could often result in depression and insecurity. Who the hell needs that as a child in their formative years! But of course, we also had our share of the the real "Eager Beavers". These kids were generally programmed by their respective Stage Mothers to approach everything with a "no nonsense", stand-offish attitude. We were "the enemy" to them, and in particular, their Mothers. The pressure brought on these kids by their Stage Mothers must have made lots of psychiatrists rich in later years. I can tell you from later experience as a Director, Stage Mothers were a royal pain in the "you know what". Overbearing, pushy, and incredibly annoying are just a few terms that come to mind. When directing, I rarely allowed mothers on the set, and in the case of infants, hired a nurse to be present, to set any "anxious" moms' minds at ease.

As I mentioned earlier, I don't think they were casting the part of "Archie" in that particular session. It can get pretty confusing trying to separate the vocal types. I think they perhaps had already decided on a voice for "Archie", then looked for a different vocal quality for "Jughead". In Radio, it was important that the "listener" could clearly identify (and separate) the voice of each Character based on tone, pitch, and perhaps even a distinct or unique style when delivering lines. The listener at home must be able to immediately register who is speaking during the broadcast, or confusion reigns supreme in their minds eye, and they would have difficulty following the story and interaction between characters.

During the "General" auditions, those responsible for casting decisions undoubtedly settled on a few kids whose voice and characterization they liked hearing , then arranged for a "Call Back" casting session, once that initial narrowing down process was concluded.

NOTE: After writing the above and while working on this Scene (Chapter)...A book about Charlie Mullens' life came out. Titled; "The Last Renaissance Man". In it, the author quotes Charlie as saying that he recalls having already been cast in the part of "Jughead", but that after I had auditioned, NBC decided to move him over to the part of Archie, and put me in as "Jughead". Waddayaknow! I just learned something. I beat the front runner out for the part. Darn!...I should have held out for more money. (There will be much more about Charlie later on.)

It was probably a few days later that my folks told me that NBC had phoned and wanted me back to read again. I don't think that I experienced any particular feeling of elation or excitement at the news. (Although I can't say the same for my parents). At that stage in my life, I had already spent 5 years as a Radio Performer, and was pretty well used to the Casting procedure. I knew enough by then not to get my hopes up in case I wasn't the final choice. It was just part of the routine as far as I was concerned. Had I known that it would be such a successful and long running role, representing many talent fees over many years, I might have thought quite differently at the time. But I learned early on that it never paid to be too over anxious. At least from my teenage perspective. And I'm sure that even my folks didn't realize the nature of the program that I was auditioning for, or its potential. I doubt that they were even aware of the popular Comic Book Characters that the show was based on, much less gave any thought to the programs importance to their "Fair Haired" boy's future and career.

At this point in the narrative, things are a bit blurred in my mind. I really don't remember if there were any other kids waiting outside the studio to read the day that I went back to NBC. I just remember meeting Charlie Mullen for the first time, and he and I read opposite each other. Charlie (NBC's original "Archie") was a slightly chubby and extremely affable guy. He was very animated, and threw himself into the part with enthusiasm. I had taken the tack that "Jughead" should deliver his lines in what we called a "Deadpan" approach. Laconic perhaps. To me the Comic Book Character looked "sleepy" and more that a bit "goofy"', so my "underplayed" squeaky voiced approach was apparently a good balance against Charlie's upbeat excitable characterization. At least that's undoubtedly what the brass at NBC must have decided.

One hears the word "Chemistry" bandied about fairly often nowadays. Well, we definitely fed off each other's chemistry that day. Needless to say… I got lucky… and got the part. And you get to read about it. Now we're both lucky. Ha!

I don't say I was "lucky" with any false sense of modesty. There certainly were other young performers who could have handled the role. But my lucky guess as to what I thought the "Jughead" character should sound like, and Charlie Mullen's approach to "Archie", coupled with the fact that we worked well opposite each other, gave us the inside track as it turned out.

Following our reading, we were asked to wait outside the studio for a little while. I guess that's when a bit of nervous anticipation set in. We both realized that back inside the control room, the "powers that be" were close to making a decision, and that we'd know our fate soon enough. Tony Leader stuck his head back out the studio door, and said *"O.K. guys, come on back in!*

At that point, a group of men (who had been in the control room) were sitting around the large "cast" table that was a fixture in each studio. Charlie and I were instructed to sit down opposite them… then Tony said, (with a big smile his face), *"Congratulations Boys, you got the parts!"*

Obviously, we both smiled back at the news, and mumbled our thanks, and said teenage stuff like *"Thanks Mr. Leader"* or *"that's great"*, or other obvious platitudes. We were then introduced to the other men seated around the table, (NBC Networks Sales and Programming representatives, as well as the programs writer, Carl Jampel, and Mr. Goldwater and Mr. Silberkleit, the publishers of Archie Comics. All were smiling!

146

Carl Jampel looked just as pleased as we were. I guess he needed to get a sense that the kids that were being hired would do justice to his dialogue concept for the program, and "flesh out" the Characters as he visualized them.

Tony went on to explain that NBC had high hopes for the series... that it was scheduled to be in a Saturday morning time slot... and double checked to make sure we didn't have any conflicts for that time time period. He then explained that we'd be getting contracts in the mail for the initial 13 week period, and that we'd need to get them signed by our parents as guardians. (The standard procedure for child actors who had yet to reach legal age.) I was the far side of 13. Charlie was the far side of 16.

Tony Leader went on to say that if the show was a success, the contracts would be renewable in 13 week cycles. We were given the tentative start date, and told what the weekly rehearsal schedule would be like. When asked if we had any questions, we shook our (numbed by the excitement) heads "no", and were told that he'd be back in touch with as as to when to report for duty, once all the contracts were signed. After shaking hands all around, I think Charlie and I walked out of that studio without our feet ever touching the floor.

On the subject of "Contracts", not all Radio Actors had to sign one whenever they appeared on a program. They were only required by the Networks when an actor was being hired as "Star", "Co-Star", or "Principal" cast member who had a "running" (continuous) part on a series. This obviously protected the Networks, (and Advertising Agencies if the show was sponsored) and assured the production staff that they wouldn't have to go through the time consumimg casting process if an actor wasn't

147

committed to playing the role on a weekly basis.

Here's the way contracts worked in those days. The Networks were guaranteed that their "investment" in the program was protected, and they could "lock in" a particular performer's "voice" for the run of the series. Although many times, the contracts stipulated only a 13 week period, there was usually a clause which gave the Network the right to renew the contract for an additional 13 week period, at their option, ad infinitum!

Of course, once a performer felt he had a "lock" on his part, and was reasonably indispensable, they could always negotiate for a little more money when contract renewal time came around.

As for the advertising agencies and their clients, it protected the "Sponsor's" product. Simply stated, if an actor's "voice" was identified with a particular program or "role", the sponsor needed assurance that that same "voice" was not going to be heavily identified with any competitive sponsor or product. That was sometimes referred to as "Product Conflict". It was even more of a concern in later years for TV actors and announcers. In TV, the performer's visual identity could not be seen to "pitch" or be associated with someone else's product. (That was a big "No-No!)

As far as the performers themselves were concerned, having a contract certainly had beneficial aspects for them as well. Aside from the obvious one of guaranteed talent fees over the life of the part they were hired to play, there was another equally important factor for "busy" actors. And that was, receiving ironclad and guaranteed compensation for taking themselves out of the running to play other similar parts, on other programs, in and around the same time slots.

Since the "Archie" program was slated for a Saturday mid-morning time slot, being locked into it with a contract certainly didn't interfere with members of the cast being available to play parts on any other NBC afternoon or "prime time" show... or programs on any other Network for that matter. But it definitely ruled out being hired to work on any of the other popular Saturday morning kids shows, like "Let's Pretend", "Coast to Coast on a Bus", etc. because of air time and rehearsal scheduling conflicts.

As I mentioned, most actors in "supporting" roles did not need contracts. Instead, their word was their bond, as the saying goes. Once they were booked to appear on a program (no matter if it was only two lines) and they accepted the assignment (part), they had damn well better show up. Or else they soon got a bad rep in the business, and incurred the displeasure of the director that hired them. It was the kiss of death to antagonize a director if you ever wanted to work for them again.

The American Federation of Radio Artists (AFRA) basic union agreement, stipulated, among other things, that once an actor accepted an assignment and was booked, we were bound to perform, or else face sanctions by the Union. This was the plus side of having a Union Affiliation as far as the Networks were concerned. However, "Scheduling Conflicts" often created problems for the performers. It was either a feast or a famine.

The word" conflict" that I used earlier had a much different connotation for performers, when it was applied to the phrase "Scheduling Conflict." In that context, it applied to a situation when an actor was offered a role on two different programs, (around the same time period) which meant the actor found himself "up the creek" without the proverbial paddle. They were then faced with the extremely difficult decision as to which program to turn down. Sometimes, the decision was based solely on economic terms. If one show was "sustaining" (non sponsored), with significantly lower talent fees, and the other a "sponsored" program paying much more, it doesn't take a Rocket Scientist to figure out which show they accepted.

Ah! therein lies the rub. The decision was not always that simple. Very often, a lot of "What If's" complicated the decision making process. Consider for a moment these all too frequent (but very real), possibilities. Let's call the lower paying sustaining program show "A", and the higher paying sponsored program show "B".

What If: Program A was being done by a director that the actor had never worked for before, and he was thrilled to finally be called by that director so he could demonstrate just how good an actor he or she was, and perhaps be called for other episodes in the future. Do you go for the "Big Break" that was finally offered, or the bigger talent fee on show "B"?

What If: The part on show "A" might well be for a character that might be written into the script on a regular basis? Is a bird in hand (fat payday for show "B") really worth more than the other long running part that might possibly be hiding in the bush?

What if: The Director of show "A" was responsible for a lot of other programs, and you wanted to stay in his good graces. But then too, maybe you also needed to make brownie points with the Director of show "B"?

See what I mean? It sometimes boiled down to playing

Russian Roulette, or which "Door" ? The Lady or the Tiger bit.

Another form of scheduling conflict that added to an actor's dilemna was even more frustrating. Those situations occured when a performer was called to do two different shows that "aired " on two different days, <u>BUT</u> the day and time of rehearsal schedules conflicted. One hated to lose a job under those circumstances.

The busier and more "popular" performers were often locked into starring roles or long running parts, so having to turn down work because of any type of scheduling conflict was not all that traumatic for them. But the rank and file actor hated to lose out on a chance to get an additional talent fee. With the amount of competition in the industry, jobs were not all that easy to come by.

Consequently, Actors went to great lengths to try and "work around" scheduling conflicts . Imagine this scenario; an actor accepts a small part in a show for 4 PM on a Thursday. Rehearsal time prior to the show was probably set for three hours ahead of air time. That meant the actor was tied up and "out of commission" for at least 4-5 hours when you factor in a half hour for getting to and from the studio. He is out of the running for any other job offers during that time frame.

Imagine also, if you will, that the same Actor in this scenario receives another call <u>after</u> accepting the original assignment. But unfortunately, it's for a program that rehearses around the same time as the first one. ONLY THIS 2nd BOOKING IS FOR A MAJOR ROLE, AND POSSIBLY A GOOD "MEATY" PART THAT MIGHT HAVE A LONG RUN ON THIS "OTHER". PROGRAM. (Maybe something that he had previously auditioned for the preceding week.) Talk about being caught between a rock and a hard place. An Actor's nightmare to say the least.

He or She was left with only two choices. One, honor the first commitment, (choking back sobs) or try to get out of it. Or, the best solution of all, work around the scheduling conflicts and do both jobs.

And yes, there were ways of getting around the problem, particularly if the performer was well known, and well liked. (Primarily, they needed to be well liked by the two different Directors involved.)

The initial option would be to contact the Director of the first show, explain the predicament, and ask if he could be released from his original commitment. Ordinarily, if it was only a small part, the director would have no problem substituting someone else out of the vast N.Y. Talent Pool. Most directors were pretty decent guys. (As was the occassional female director). They understood the nature of the business, and if they liked you, they didn't mind making minor concessions like this. However, one had better not go to the well too many times asking for favors. The director would soon tire of the game, and not bother to cast you anymore if you weren't reliable.

The other option. After talking the problem over with the two directors involved, the performer would try and fit both programs into his schedule. Sometimes it involved the actor in question hiring a "stand in" (with the director's permission if it was a minor part), who would read the lines in rehearsal. Then, the "real" actor would show up to do the actual broadcast. Once the first show was out of the way, they would rush to the other studio to perform on the second show. Really no big deal, provided both programs were broadcast on the same network. Using NBC as as example, the principal studios were located on the 3rd, 6th and 8th floors of 30 Rockefeller Center, the huge building shown below. (The NBC complex was located in the circled area) No big problem even if it meant taking an elevator to get between studios.

NOTE: That preceeding photograph is a very old shot. The NYC skyline has changed dramatically over the years.

But pity the poor actor who was cast in a show on NBC, and another program following on CBS,quite a few city blocks apart.

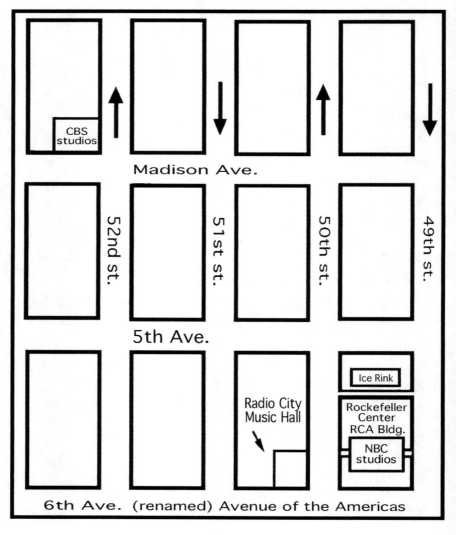

NBC, located at 30 Rockefeller Plaza, was located between 49th and 50th street. Rockefeller Center stretched all the way between 5th and 6th Avenues. Crosstown streets alternated in "one way" directions. (East and West), and North South for the "Avenues". Back then, Avenues permitted travel in both directions.

The distance between the Avenues was probably twice as far as the distance between the streets. This bit of useless information comes in handy to fully understand what follows next.

CBS (see wonderful map not drawn to scale) was located at 485 Madison Ave. on the corner of 52nd street. To get there from NBC, (or visa versa) one had to traverse from the 50th street exit of NBC, close to the 6th Ave. end of the building, head east, cross 5th ave. to get to the next main Avenue, Madison, then go north 2 blocks to 52st street.

If you are reasonably proficient in math, you would say, heck, that's just a short stroll of 4 city blocks. But because crosstown streets were so long, it was the equivelant distance of 6 very long city blocks.

Consequently, if an actor was at NBC and needed to get to CBS quickly for another show they were booked for, (with no time to spare), they only had two choices.

If you were young, you could run like hell, and be totally out of breath when you got there, or... take a taxi. (Back in the '40's and '50's, the streets in NY were not gridlocked like they are today, so a cab had a good chance of travelling that distance in a reasonably short period of time, and one arrived without being exhausted. Since East Bound 50th street was one way for vehicals,

155

one could easily zip East over to Madison, and then a quick left turn to 52nd in the span of 5 or 10 minutes, door to door. On more than a few occasions, you would see an Actor literally race down the halls of NBC to the elevator bank. There, an accomplice would be stationed, holding an elevator for him, (after a generous tip to the operator). Once the elevator decended to the main floor, the actor would dash out of the building using NBC's 50th street entrance (note the Radio City Music Hall marquee in the lower right of the photograph below).

Outside, a 2nd accomplice would be waiting with a taxicab, motor running, door open (and, of course, meter running). The "Cabbie", aware that his fare was a radio actor in a big hurry to get to CBS, would agree to rush over there. After all, he was now a vital part of "Show Biz".

There then ensued a wild cab ride across town to CBS, where the reverse elevator process would take place when the actor scampered into that building, and up to the studio floors. Usually, this "mad dash" only occurred with the "bigger names" in the industry, and the more popular actors, who were in great demand because of their talent.

It wasn't all that easy to get to WOR Mutual Broadcasting.

The distance was far greater (those studios were much further downtown), so an actor performing on either CBS or NBC couldn't get to WOR in time for a program that was in close proximity to those on the other Networks. I recall WOR was around 40th St. and Broadway. A distance of at least 12 blocks from NBC and 16 blocks from CBS.

Before leaving the subject of NBC's location, no brief tour would be complete without this photograph.

In the lower center, we have the statue that we lovingly called "Golden Boy" looking down on Rockefeller Centers fabled Ice Rink. In the summertime, the rink was converted back to a lovely outdoor terrace resturant. The equally famous Rockefeller Center annual Christmas tree can be seen right above the statue, and the East entrance to NBC is in the building immediately to the left of the tree. The tree is not lighted, or decorated, so the time frame must be sometime in November.

I spent untold hours in my young lifetime hanging over the upper walls that bordered the rink, killing time between jobs or auditions, watching people make fools of themselves trying to make like some star of the Ice Capades. But I only watched if the winter chill factor was in the moderate range. I think I even put skates on a few times myself, but why make a fool of myself in front of all those gaping tourists.

Tours over. Back to work.

Since the vast majority of my radio appearances were on NBC, (once the "Archie Andrews" program started), I didn't have any major conflict problems on Saturday mornings. But as I said, the "Archie" cast members were definitely out of the running for any further appearances on "Let's Pretend" or "Coast to Coast on a Bus".

O.K. Where was I before I got sidetracked and talked about "Contracts 'n Conflicts" and gave you a lesson in the Geographic layout of the NY Radio Actor's Playground.

Oh yeah! Charlie Mullen and yours truly just got hired to play two "Plum" parts starring in a new series over theNBC Network. Heady stuff!

While we both waited on our contracts, Tony Leader finished holding auditions for the rest of the "Principals" in the cast. "Betty", "Veronica", and "Archie's" Mom and Dad, "Mary and Fred Andrews." In all liklihood, casting was also started for other

"Archie" comic book characters who might be needed to make an occasional appearance on the show, such as Mr. Weatherbee, the High School principal, Miss Grundy, the teacher, Reggie Mantle, the rich-kid nemesis of Archie, etc.

In the meantime, Leo Kampinski, the Musical Director of the NBC Orchestra, was busy writing the opening theme music for the program, and Carl Jampel (writer) was obviously busy churning out more scripts for the series. I'm not certain what process NBC went through to select Carl Jampel to pen the scripts, or what his Radio credits were before doing the "Archie" show. But over the entire run of the program, he probably turned out well over 500 episodes.........Now, Let the show begin.

But First!... A few words from our Sponsor.

Drat! Old habits die hard. Well, at least you've earned another intermission before Act 3.

INTERMISSION

OK! We have no scenery changes to make since we are in the era of Radio Broadcasting. This particular intermission serves only one purpose. It adds a few more pages to the length of the book so the Author can charge more money for it. Shameful behavior.

Besides, Intermissions in radio were not necessary, unless you count the commercials that occurred in the middle of the program. But they hardly gave one time to stretch their legs and get some refreshment. Ah! But no problem. With radio entertainment, all one had to do was raise the sound level of the home radio, and go into the kitchen, (or powder room if necessary) and not miss a thing.

At no extra charge, you can do the same thing with this book. No. I don't mean raise the volume. (Unless you are the type that reads out loud.) Just carry it with you if you are so engrossed and can't put it down.

However, as a public service presented by the optometrists of this country, we suggest you pause, close your eyes momentarily, then, start reading anew. We certainly don't want to be guilty of causing you any undue eyestrain because the book is holding you captive and you just can't wait to find out what happens in the final Act. Three more scenes to go. No fair peeking.

But since the pages that follow will contain some reference to early live TV, I suppose something should be said about the duration of Commercial breaks on television. In the good old days of live TV, commercial time was limited to just a few minutes per half-hour. A long standing advertising formula that was borrowed from Radio sponsorship. You had to hurry to the refrigerator or you might miss something important.

Nowadays, you can practically walk the dog, then build a Triple-Decker sandwich, (and even consume it) before they finished stringing all the TV ads back to back. And to think I was a party to all that by becoming a Director of TV Commercials later on in life. Mea Culpa.

But like I said earlier, that's a totally different book.

Times up! Let's get back to the "Kinder, Gentler Age" that was reasonably free of Commercial clutter.

Act 3

Scene 1

(Music) "Friendship, Friendship......What a perfect Blendship"

(Establish music, then fade under)

(CUE NARRATION)

From the moment that the entire cast was assembled for our first "Archie" program's rehearsal, it was obvious that it was going to be a very pleasant experience. Being the youngest, (at 13+), I was definitely made to feel like one of the "grown ups" and treated with respect and warmth by my fellow cast members. That same camaraderie existed between all the regular cast members and the programs writer, Carl Jampel, as well as the many directors we had over the program's 9 year lifespan. I recall we had at least 6 different directors over that period. Some only remained at the programs helm for a year. One in particular remained with the show for many years. More about them later.

The bottom line. Everyone was a seasoned " Pro". I always approached my job in a very professional manner, thanks to my prior years of training in the theatre and numerous other radio programs. That's all anyone ever really cared about. As long as someone was totally professional and held up their end (along with the rest of the cast), they were admired and respected in our business. Race, religion, national origin, were never really considerations in the Radio Acting fraternity. (In later years, however, political ideology did infect our tight knit Broadcasting community.) It even touched a cast member of the "Archie" show. A really neat guy who played "Archie's" father.

Before going any further, I need to make a disclaimer to avoid confusion. From now on, when I mention an actor who was the "First" Archie, or the "First" Betty, or the first "Mr. Andrews", I will be referring to the NBC network version of "The Adventures of Archie Andrews" that began in 1945, and ran continuously for the next nine years.

But I would be remiss (and selfish) if I didn't mention that the Archie Comic Book characters had an even earlier start as a radio program. But I was not involved, and frankly, knew nothing about it until someone clued me in many years after the fact. To begin with, researchers tell me that in 1943, it was first attempted as a 15 minute daily show every weekday on NBC's "Blue" Network.

Huh? What's the Blue Network you ask?

Unless one is a died in the wool Old Time Radio fan and into the OTR hobby of collecting recordings of those old programs, I need to briefly explain the radio broadcasting "Network" system. (It operates in much the same way as the TV networks do today.)

Radio "Networks" were basically an affiliation of a whole bunch of "Local" radio stations throughout the United States. These individual radio stations serviced the local markets and broadcast programs in their specific regions. The geographic range

164

(distance) of their broadcast signals depended on the "power" of their transmitters, and the height of their antennas. Obviously, the denser the population (more people) in any given area, meant that they could charge more for advertising, because they were "delivering" more listeners to the client. Simply stated, they could offer "More Bang for the Buck".

The "Prime" markets were the major cities throughout the country. All radio stations, to survive, relied on local advertising to meet their overhead and operating costs. For the most part, the smaller markets could not afford to produce quality radio shows and professional entertainment. In addition, the talent pool of professional actors, writers, musicians, could only be found in the major cities, which afforded those individuals far greater opportunities to earn a living.

Consequently, the source of original programing material (entertainment) originated in a few key cities that could afford to produce the shows; Primarily, New York, Detroit, Chicago and Los Angeles. And in these major markets, there was usually more than one station. Competition was fierce. It was important for each station to offer programming (shows) that people wanted to hear, to lure the listener away from the competition.

Since the smaller towns and stations were unable to produce the quality of programming that was originating from the major cities, "Networking" was invented. Let's take NBC as an example. They would offer these smaller stations the opportunity to carry (broadcast) the programs that originated from the NBC stations in the major cities. That meant many more people could hear the programs. Then, NBC could say to an advertiser, If you sponsor such and such a program, we can deliver your sales message to "skaty eight" million people, ("households", to use the advertising term), in 50 to 60 (whatever) markets throughout the country.

These local stations usually had a contractual arrangement with NBC to become a part of the "Network". They were then referred to as NBC Network Affiliates. (CBS , Mutual and ABC had similar arrangements). The contracts specified that these local stations would carry all the radio programs that NBC produced, in specific "high listenership" time periods, with options to pick up other program offerings as well.

In return for carrying the NBC program in their local area, these stations benefited in two ways. The first was the fact that they were supplied high quality programming throughout the day to entertain and attract listeners. They then would sell local advertising in the station breaks between the shows.

Secondly, in the specific time periods each day that they were contractually obligated to carry NBC programs, they received a modest fee if it was a commercially sponsored show. Then too, during the popular evening prime time period, they could also run commercials during the station breaks, and charge more for those ads, because the listenership was much higher.

Broadcasting Networks were a win-win situation all around. NBC could claim a vast audience because these locally owned stations throughout the country broadcast the shows that NBC originated. That in turn enabled NBC to attract national advertisers to sponsor those programs. The local stations made money on fees for carrying those shows, and from their own local advertising revenue. This gave the local stations some operating capital to produce their own local programs during the periods that they were not obligated to carry the NBC shows. Obvious programming fare would be local news, farm reports, Sunday religious shows, and in some cases, even local entertainment.

Without delving into this "network" system much further, I should at least point out that the National Broadcasting Company owned their own NBC stations in each of the major markets. As did CBS. They were called "O&O" (Owned and Operated) stations, in markets like New York, Detroit, Chicago, Los Angeles. That's why some of the famous NBC programs of that period were not produced solely from NBC's New York studios. They could just as easily originate from NBC's O&O studios in those other major cities, and fed over the entire Network that way.

O.K. Can I get off the technical stuff, and get on with the explanation about why the "Archie" show was first aired on the NBC's "Blue" network as early as 1943?

In those days, NBC actually had two different networks. (Don't ask me why.) One was identified as the "Blue" network, the other was called the "Red". Each of them had their own roster of programs. NBC's fierce competition for listenership and advertising dollars was the Columbia Broadcasting System (CBS), and the Mutual Broadcasting System. (We knew it by its NY local station call letters, WOR.)

For some reason or another, the Federal Government agency responsible for radio broadcasting decided that the National Broadcasting Company had to divest itself of one of its networks, so sometime in 1944/45, NBC kept the "Red" network, and it became plain old NBC. NBC's former "Blue" network was spun off and became the American Broadcasting Company (ABC). Mutual

Broadcasting just plodded along trying to compete with those other two broadcasting "giants".

Ok, here's what I learned about those earlier attempts at producing a series based on the "Archie" comic book characters. It seems that at some point in 1943, NBC developed a version of the show in a 15 minute daily format on NBC "Blue". But that only lasted for four months. Then it was switched to a once a week half hour format on Friday evenings. However, it remained in that new time slot on the "Blue" network for only two months until the end of 1943.

Then a major switcheroo occurred. The show was dropped entirely from the NBC "Blue" network lineup and was next heard on WOR Mutual for a period of about 5 months (early to mid 1944). No one I've talked to can recall the reason for the switch in networks. It could be that WOR offered Archie Comic Publications more money for the rights to use the characters, or that NBC had other programming ideas. But it could also have been an even more devious reason, seeing as how NBC got the show back a year later.

Perhaps NBC decided to strip the show from the "Blue" network so it would not be part of the program lineup when the Blue network shows became ABC network property. Maybe the powers that be decided to keep the show on the air, made a deal with Mutual, and it went back to a 15 minute five-a-week serial format on the Mutual network until June 1944.

But then, strangely, it was off the air for an entire year. Perhaps NBC needed that time to consolidate their program schedules because of the big NBC "Red" and "Blue" network changeover.

All I know is that when it came back to NBC in mid June of 1945, it was a whole new show. None of the original cast members of those earlier programs were utilized. The program had a fresh start, and in a totally different time period. It became, and remained, the mainstay of NBC's Saturday morning kid's programs. The 10:30 AM time slot was ideal for the 6 to 14 age range that the comic book targeted, and the growth in popularity of both the radio show and comic book went hand in hand.

Again, in all fairness, I should salute my fellow actors and actresses who pioneered the roles in those early years. But just very briefly because details and records from those early years are sketchy at best. Besides, this book is about my years playing Jughead. Let 'em write their own book. (Just kidding folks.)

My thanks to Elizabeth McLeod, and Jay Hickerson, (two highly respected Old Time Radio research experts) who furnished me with the following names. Burt Boyer was listed as having played "Archie" in one of the earlier versions.

 And as I mentioned earlier in the book, I know that Jack Grimes (on the left) played Archie, and Cameron Andrews played Jughead on WOR Mutual.

Unfortunately, I don't have pictures of the other cast members, but the names given me were Joy Geffen as "Betty", Vivian Smolen as "Veronica", "Archie's" mother and father, "Mr. and Mrs. Andrews" were played by Peggy Allenby and Reese Taylor.

Now! That said... Can I talk about the "new" Archie show?

On the following pages, meet the
"Archie" comic book characters
that the radio show was based on
and gave the actors "inspiration".

Again, my thanks to the publishers of Archie Comics for permission to use the comic book artwork. The thumbnail profiles of the characters were extracted from an 2001 Archie Comics press release.

THE CAST OF CHARACTERS

Archie Andrews

Everyone's favorite teen-ager from Riverdale, is generous, well-mannered, but extremely impulsive. It is the impulsiveness that usually gives him cause for regret as he enters into and out of teenage dilem-mas.

One of the most important characteristics of Archie is his susceptibility to the feminine charm. For more than 60 years, he has been caught in the middle of one of America's most famous love triangles be-tween Betty and Veronica. His adventures in trying to choose one of the two have always gotten him into trouble.

(Authors note: What's that expression? "Life imitates art".)

Jughead Jones

Jughead Jones is Archie's best friend. His real name is Forsythe; however, Jughead seems to fit his personality better. He, along with his famous dog, Hot Dog, are constantly joining Archie in his misadventures.

Jughead is well known for his favorite activities: eating, sleeping, and eating again. Whether it be hamburgers, hot dogs or pizza, Jughead won't be found without food nearby. It is then that he is at his happiest. When not eating or helping Archie out of a mess, he has been seen hiding from Ethel, who is constantly seeking his affection.

(Authors note: There were a few minor deviations from the comic book Jughead and the Radio version. We didn't use Jughead's dog on radio, and in our case, the gal always chasing Jughead was named "Agatha".)

Betty Cooper

Betty is your average small-town girl, wholesome, sweet, and extremely devoted to Archie. Unfortunately, the beautiful blond teen often has to play second-fiddle to Veronica and her schemes to win Archie's love. But through it all, Betty remains completely unaffected and loyal to Archie. She is very intelligent, hard working, and continues to challenge Archie as he must choose which girl he really wants.

Veronica Lodge

Gorgeous, sophisticated, and very RICH. Veronica has no problem with the boys, except maybe Archie. She is forever trying to win over his heart and will stop at almost nothing to prove to him that she is the right choice. The sexy brunette is very conceited, usually fickle, and extremely flirtatious; whether using her money or her looks, some day she hopes to obtain the one thing she can't buy… Archie.

(Authors note: The next two characters were featured heavily in the radio program, but try as I might, I couldn't find the comic book character profiles for them in the material that ACP sent me. But I'm fairly certain that my description will mirror their comic book persona.)

Fred Andrews Archie's long suffering father. Continually perplexed and frustrated by having to deal with Archie and his friends misadventures. It seems that his desire to maintain "peace and quiet" in the Andrews household was continually at risk, and virtually impossible. As were his attempts to get projects done around the house without Archie (or Jughead) inadvertently messing them up.

Mary Andrews Warm, gracious, and a caring mother. And somewhat of a steadying influence on the family, particularly her husband. Mrs. Andrews continually provided the impetus to get her spouse (and/or Archie) working on a task that she wanted accomplished, or involve them in some sort of family activity.

(Authors note: With the usual messed up results.)

174

Mr. Lodge Veronica's very wealthy father. He does not support his daughter's flirtation with Archie. It seems every time he turns his back, Archie has done something to disrupt his personal and professional life.

(Authors note: Although Mr. Lodge is featured prominently in the Comic Book stories, and is constantly being irritated by Archie, he was rarely used in the radio version. That was due primarily to the fact that on radio, Archie's father was the primary foil and recipient for all of Archie's misadventures, consequently another antagonist wasn't necessary. Not only that, it probably was a budgetary consideration by the NBC brass to minimize talent fees.)

Mrs. Lodge Veronica's rather haughty and social climbing mother. A pillar in the community, and much involved in charitable works. And unlike her husband, quite possibly perceives Archie as a tolerable member of the lower class.

(Authors note: Mrs. Lodge's character was used more frequently in the radio version, but more often than not, as intimidation of sorts for Archie's father),

175

Reggie Mantle Reggie is the ultimate wiseguy, always looking to put a fast one over on someone, usually Archie. Reggie is very handsome and an all-around athlete. He believes that he is the best at everything. Reggie is Archie's arch rival in almost every endeavor, especially where Veronica is concerned. He may outsmart Archie with his tricks, but neither of them ever seem to win in the end.

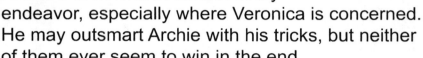

Mr. Weatherbee The principal of Riverdale High School. His short temper leaves very little patience for Archie and Jugheads recurring pranks.

Miss Grundy Archie's well known teacher at Riverdale High. She tends to be strict, but underneath it all she is a good-natured person.

Over the years, the pages of Archie Comics featured many more characters in the story lines that interrelated with Archie. Such as "Pop Tate" who owned the soda parlor hangout that the teenagers frequented, and "Big Moose", the "muscle-head" of the crowd. But as I mentioned earlier, radio program budget restraints kept the cast members down to a realistic number each week.

The regular radio cast members that were featured on every program were always; Archie, Jughead, Betty, Veronica and Mr. & Mrs. Andrews. But that's not to say other actors weren't used as story lines and plots dictated. That was particularly true in the early days when the show was getting established. Mr. Weatherbee and Miss Grundy were often written into the scripts, as were other supporting cast members who portrayed everything from the cop on the beat, sales clerks, trades people, Doctors, etc. Not to mention the Fat Lady from the circus sideshow. (That was an experience). The radio Jughead even had a dippy Uncle Herman that would show up from time to time.

Then too, when the program was sponsored, (Kraft Cheese and Swifts Meats) the production budgets were more generous, consequently, more characters could be written into the scripts. But in the twilight years of radio (the early 50's), when TV was sounding the death knell for radio entertainment, particularly for the sustaining (non sponsored) programs, the Archie show held on tenaciously; due primarily to it's young fan base. But it meant minimizing the overhead (talent fees) and required the writer to create story lines that just needed the 6 main characters.

But this book is not about the decline of radio entertainment. It is meant to celebrate those years when radio was "king", and I was once a prince (Let's Pretend) but wound up a "Jughead."

Authors Note: As I stated earlier in the acknowledgement section of the book, I owe many thanks to Charlie Mullen for helping fill in my teenage memory blanks from that period. One Q & A session with him involved a 2 hour phone call. Bless him, Charlie had a mind like a steel trap, and it was always great fun to reminisce with him.

I don't recall working with any of the older cast members prior to that opening day, but we soon became a very tight knit "family" and definitely enjoyed the comradeship and interaction when we spent about 4 hours a week together in the studio.

And the two young girls playing "Betty" and "Veronica", boy… were they ever cute. Charlie liked teasing me about them. He thought I had a crush on them. Well… maybe just a small one.

By way of introduction, the cover page of a typical script (opposite) lists the "live" characters who played those comic book characters when our version of the show first started.

"The Adventures of
Archie Andrews"

Episode #1   6/10/45*

DIRECTOR...Anton Leder
WRITER...Carl Jample

CAST

Archie..Charlie Mullen
Jughead...Harlan Stone
Mr. Andrews..Vinton Hayworth
Mrs. Andrews...Alice Yourman
Veronica..Gloria Mann
Betty...Doris Grundy

Musical Conductor..................................Leo Kampinski
Studio Engineer......................................"Doc" ?
Sound Effects...Sam Malone

* A fictitious date, because I can only remember the year.

Charlie Mullen brought a unique teenage exuberance to the role of Archie. He didn't have to play "young"...He was young!!! At 16, he probably was the perfect age when we started. He gave the character a certain naivete, a sort of childlike innocence. And whenever the story line called for Archie to lose his cool over some sort of mishap, Charlie would throw his whole body into it. Lots of agitation and arm flailing. And he didn't have a studio audience to entertain with those antics. (We started having studio audiences about a year after the show started.) Exaggerated movement just helped him reach the level of teenage excitability or frustration that the dialogue called for.

Now I ask you? Can you see the resemblence between the bright eyed and bushy tailed comic book face, and the one Charlie brought to the party? And we certainly did have a party. We had a lot of fun working together. And we got paid for it too. A couple of young kids being silly and throwing ourselves into our work.

As for me, I was just about to turn 14, and could keep up with Charlie's happy-go-lucky teenage antics. Being silly came with the territory. And Charlie provided a great counterpoint for my interpretation of the "Jughead" role. When I saw the way that character was drawn in the comic books, it gave me a clue as to how he might sound. Jughead rarely had his his eyes open. And, he almost always had a downturn to his mouth. I saw him as low key, laid back, and a slightly sarcastic guy with a very dry sense of humor. I tried to convey that with my voice. I thought the character needed to sound a little goofy (like he looked) and added a squeak to my voice whenever Jughead got excited.

Now I ask you? Can you see the resemblence between the sleepy eyed and "goofy" expression of the comic book face and the one I brought to the party? (If you say yes, I'll never forgive you.) But when it came to posing for the NBC Publicity department, I tried to look the part.

When I look back on those days, I recall that whenever I was introduced to kids my age, and someone would bring up the fact that I played "Jughead" on the radio, they would invariably say. *"Gee, you don't look like Jughead"*. (To which I replied… *"Thank You"*!) What the hell else was I supposed to say? But if I had a nickle for everytime I heard that, I wouldn't have had to write this book to make a buck in my old age. ☺

I think at this point I'll introduce the rest of our original cast, then fill the reader in on their backgrounds and later careers. At least, what I can recall about those who stayed in the "business".

I don't know if it was by design, or by accident, but the two young females first cast, each bore a resemblence to their comic

181

book counterparts. At least as far as hair coloring was concerned.

Doris Grundy was a charming and very likable young lady, (a somewhat tall, pretty, and slender blond), just like the character "Betty" she played.

But for some strange reason, Doris only played the part for about a year. Something came up that prompted her to leave New York. I seem to recall that she was California bound, and I heard that she eventually went into producing films on the west coast. But don't quote me on that. It was something I just learned recently after talking to Bob Hastings. (If you don't know who he is, you will soon learn.) As to her earlier credits before getting the part of "Betty", I don't have a clue. I think she was a small town girl, new to the "big city", and relatively new to performing. But she was good at it, and a welcome member of the cast.

Gloria Mann, our first "Veronica", was another equally delightful and pretty young gal. And guess what? She was a brunette just like the comic book beauty she portrayed.

(ooops! I'm gonna get in trouble for using a politically incorrect word.) Apparently, in today's world, the feminists will come down on me hard for referring to Gloria (or any female) as a "Pretty gal". Sigh! Life was so much easier in that earlier era. Back then, young ladies didn't mind that term. It was simply a contraction of the word "Girl". But even that term is frowned on today. Gee! Think of all the old songs that are probably banned nowadays. "My Gal Sal" , "Buffalo Gals", "I want a Gal just like the gal that married dear old dad. Etc.Etc. Oh well! Pardon my lack of propriety. My only excuse…"You can't teach an old dog new tricks".

Have you discovered another problem that comes with age? I can digress and change the subject at the drop of a hat. But I'm happy to report that I can remember exactly where we left off. We were discussing a very pretty woman (young lady, female person, whatever) named Gloria Mann. Gloria was slightly older than Doris, (or perhaps she just seemed that way) because she had been in the business for a few years prior to joining our cast and seemed more "sophisticated". And in addition, she wore lots of makeup, so she looked older and more "worldly". Dare I say Sexier? Perfect for playing the comic book vamp "Veronica". And Gloria played the part with a put-on Southern Bell accent that made the voices of the two girls very distinct. As I mentioned earlier, a definite must for radio performers. A totally different vocal quality made the characters more readily identifiable to the "ear" of the listener whenever they were in the same scene together.

Gloria's earlier radio credits, before being cast on "Archie", included a running part on the Soap Opera, "The Life & Love of Dr. Susan". I'm sure she did other work during the many years she played "Veronica" on our show, but the names of the programs are not known to me. I'm sure the other members of the cast paid

183

attention to what everyone else was working on back then, but I was in my post puberty "teenager" mode. Sorry!

To lovely Alice Yourman goes the honor of being the only original cast member to play "Mrs. Andrews for the entire 9 years the show was on the air. Except for occasional ill health, that is.

184

For that reason alone, she deserves having her photograph prominately displayed in this narrative. I'm sure you'd agree that she was quite lovely. And her warmth and charm was certainly the equal of her beauty.

Alice could always be counted on to bring great range to her charactization of "Mary Andrews". She could play the caring Mother to the hilt, but could be acceptably stern (without sounding shrewish) when it came to bringing order out of chaos. "Archie", or her husband "Fred Andrews", would bend to her will by her character's use of guile, reverse psychology, and vocal intimidation when necesary.

On a personal note, Alice was always friendly, solicitous, and exuded a great deal of warmth. She was like a second "Mom" to me over the many years we worked together. But when it came to rehearsing and on air performance, she was all business. Years later, I was thrilled to be able to use her in TV commercials.

Alice Yourman's other notable radio credits included a stint on CBS's "Two on a Clue" during 1944/46 as the 'Announcer". She also had appearances on a show called "Secret Missions". In 1946, one of her other starring roles was as "Myrt" on "Myrt and Marge" when that program went into syndication. She was teamed with Vinton Hayworth on that show. (Much more about Vinton Hayworth on the next page.) Also in that cast was Cliff Arquette. (Remember him as "Charlie Weaver" from Jack Parr's TV Show?) A lifelong close friendship between Cliff Arquette and Vinton Hayworth developed from working together back then.

I regard Vinton Hayworth with great affection. Primarily because Vinton was the first "Mr. Andrews" in our cast and a fun guy to be around. He seemed to enjoy the teenage antics that Charlie and I would indulge in, and would egg us on many times. He had a great sense of humor. A very dapper and distinquished looking gentleman, don't you agree? But Vinton was not above playing practical jokes on us. He pulled a beauty that I'll tell you about later.

Actually, the only physical resemblance between Vinton and the Comic Book "Mr. Andrews" was the mustache. But I seriously doubt that he was cast in the part for that reason. Vinton had great range as an actor, and an essential ingredient for the dialogue and situatiions connected with the role he played. Actors called it "comedic timing".

Vinton amassed quite a few radio credits before he left for the west coast to work out there, and eventually co-starred on TV as the first person to play the "General" on "I Dream of Genie" (Prior to Barton MacLane assuming the role.) Some of Vinton's earlier radio shows were "The Adventures of Father Brown", "Betty and Bob", "The Chase", "It's Higgins Sir", and the very popular "Lights Out", in addition to the previously mentioned "Myrt & Marge".

I don't recall why Vinton left the cast of the show after playing Archie's father for about a year. He certainly wasn't fired. But many actors travelled back and forth between NY and LA when better job opportunities presented themselves, and perhaps Vinton had a shot at working on a prime time "sponsored" program, and jumped at the opportunity for a bigger payday.

Interestingly enough, some years later during the run of our series, Vinton was back in New York and would sometimes rejoin the cast and play other character parts. I recall he played a Doctor in one of those later episodes.

I guess that briefly covers the initial regular weekly cast members. But since Vinton Hayworth is fresh on my mind, I might as well finish up with a situation that concerned him during the Communist Blacklisting period that affected all fields of entertainment, particularly on the West Coast and the Film Industry.

I was not aware of it at the time, but there were a few NY Radio Actors who were extremely vocal about American patriotism and made no bones about it. To them, any and all Communists were enemies of our country. Much like the radical and fanatical Muslim Fundamentalists of today are considered our enemy, due to their avowed intention to "destroy" us, and are also perceived to be a very real threat to our way of life.

The treachery of Stalin after World War II, and our "Police Action" (War) against Communist North Korea and China, was certain to create a wave of patriotism much like we recently experienced after 9/11. Consequently, back then, anyone sympathetic to the "Communist" cause, or ideology, was not very popular to say the least. I can't say I blamed those patriots. Hey, I was in the Air Force during the Korean war. Communists were my enemy.

Consequently, some people made a big deal about exposing "Commies" in the entertainment industry, and Radio performers were not exempt. It's my understanding that Vinton was among the vocal cadre who made no bones about identifying Communist sympathizers, who to them, were enemies in our midst. But he was not as involved as some of the other "big" names in the radio acting fraternity. Among those that I worked with back in those days, who were even stronger advocates for the unmasking and suppression of all Communist sympathizers, were Clayton "Bud" Collier and Dwight Weist.

In my opinion, you couldn't find two nicer guys. Bud Collier's most notable radio credit was in the lead role of "Mr. District Attorney", but he also appeared on many other programs as an announcer/performer. He went on to even greater fame as a very popular game show host in television.

Dwight Weist also did a ton of work as a performer and announcer. I would be hard pressed to name two gentlemen who enjoyed as much respect among their fellow performers as they did. Not just for their professional abilities, but also due in part to their good natured personalities. That's why they could be so influential when it came to patriotic zeal.

I had a wonderful opportunity much later in life to spend some time with Vinton Hayworth a short while before his death.

My dear childhood friend Ben Cooper (who you learned about earlier), threw a big party for me during one of my visits to LA when I went out there to direct some commercials. The main purpose of the party was primarily to reunite Vinton Hayworth and me after more than 30 years, (as well as meet Ben's L.A. circle of friends). It was a delightful evening, and I had the opportunity to really talk to Vinton as one mature adult to another. I discovered a great deal about him, but the most revealing side of Vinton was his pride in his American heritage, and the sacrifices his ancestors made to "Preserve the Union". Particularly during the Civil War. He felt he owed them something, and his Anti-Communist stand had its roots in that heritage. I suppose that today, it could be excused as simply his genetic programming. I can relate to that because of my ancestral ties to the Civil War. After our reunion, Vinton sent me a lot of material he had written about the Civil War, and a wonderful calendar he designed depicting Civil War events.

Because of Vinton's friendship with Cliff Arquett, (who was an even bigger Civil war buff), I was instantly embraced by Cliff when I directed him in some commercials shortly after Vinton's death. During that shoot, we spent every moment we could talking about either Vinton or the Civil War. For those of you who may not be aware, Cliff Arquette maintained a museum at Gettysburg, and did some wonderful Civil War militaria carvings. I was in hog heaven to meet and work with that fine gentleman.

OK! that's the last you will hear from me about politics in show business, or the Civil War for that matter. But I hope it fleshes out the human side of some of the people I had the honor to work with over the years.

Now, lets get back to 1945, and some fun stuff.

There would often be occasions when other " Archie" comic book characters would be written into the scripts, but not necessarily on a weekly basis.

One of our favorite actors who would often join our happy group was a cultured, well dressed elderly gentleman named Arthur Maitland. Arthur played "Mr. Weatherbee" (the Riverdale High School principal) to the hilt. Unfortunately, I couldn't locate a photograph of this distinguised looking gentelman who actually wore pince-nez glasses, but he was a genius at playing the part with what I would term "flustered bluster". The antics of Archie and Jughead invariably would cause "Mr. Weatherby" to lose his cool, and Arthur Maitland brought to the show a unique breathy vocal quality that almost sounded like he was being asphyxiated when his character became upset. I don't recall anyone else playing that role during the life of the program, but it's possible. It's just that in my opinion, the role belonged to him alone because he lived the part.

The other Riverdale High character that is featured so heavily in the Comic Book, and who we also used in the show on occasion, was the teacher "Miss Grundy". Over the years, no one actress in particular played or "owned" that role. There were any number of performers that graced our stage playing Miss Grundy. Invariably, whenever we had a change in directors, you could count on someone new (that the director was particular fond of), to be called for the part. I don't mean fond of them in the romantic sense. But fond of their talent, having used them earlier on other programs. Only the 6 regular cast members had performance contracts with NBC, and anytime a new director came along, he was stuck with us. Happily, none of them seemed to mind. And, when they discovered that we were all pros and good in the parts we played, they would often hire us to work on some of their other program assignments.

One such actress was a woman named Rolly Bester. Rolly was well liked in the industry, and could play a wide range of characters. She could play Miss Grundy one week, and a nurse in the doctors office a few weeks later. Versatility in our business was paramount. Obviously, to be able to change one's vocal quality meant being called for a wider range of character parts. But I suppose the fact that Rolly was such a sultry beauty, in addition to being talented, didn't hurt any. But being a teenager, all I could do is look…and dream.

But!!! When I eventually matured (you'll have to trust me on that), Rolly and I became good friends in my later directorial days. She eventually left the performing end of the business, (probably for the same reasons I did), and became a successful casting director with one of the major NY advertising agencies. As a matter of fact, Rolly made a point of introducing me to a number of TV commercial producers at her Ad agency, and I got some of my earlier Directorial assignments thru her contacts. I loves ya Rolly. You're a class act.

One of my other really favorite people was Joan Shay. In my old age, we met up again at an Old Time Radio Convention in New York. I was able to confide to her (after all these years) that I had a big crush on her back in those good old days. Call it harmless teenage infatuation, but Joan was charming, good looking, exuded warmth, and had a smile

that would melt the coldest heart. Not to mention a great bod. Joan was often used on the program, in a variety of roles.

Not only was she closely identified with playing snooty "Mrs. Lodge", Veronica's mother, but whenever Alice Yourman (Mrs. Andrews) was ill or needed to be absent, Joan always was the first choice as Alice's temporary replacement. She added great chemistry to the cast

In all the years the program was on the air, I don't recall ever having a personality clash or conflict between any of the 6 regular cast members, or for that matter, with any of the other numerous performers that were hired to play all sorts of Characters. And when one of the principals had to leave the show, (as in the case of our first "Archie" and shortly after that, our original "Betty"), the new arrivals instantly became "family" and we didn't lose a beat. That's due to the skill of the directors at finding someone who filled their shoes perfectly.

I'll get to the "newbies" in a minute, but first I have to finish telling you about about the early years.

The above is obviously a staged photograph for the benefit of the NBC Publicity department. No one is even coming close to working on the correct side of the microphone.

But it's a cute shot of Doris Grundy, Vinton Hayworth and Gloria Mann.The setting is the original NBC studio that we used.

Did I mention that in the early days of the program (maybe the first year) we had a live studio band doing our music? (The opening and closing theme and musical "bridges" between scenes). Our original conductor, (and composer of the programs theme) was the head of the NBC Studio Orchestra, Leo Kampinski. (Not to be confused with the NBC Symphony Orchestra.). Later Milt Katims, his assistant, took over directing the band until we switched over to an organist, the wonderful and very talented George Wright.

Since the program was not commercially sponsored for the first few years, that probably was a cost saving move by the network. Milt Katims eventually went from NBC to bigger and better things. According to Charlie Mullen (my official memory freshen-upper), Milt Katims became the Director of the Seattle Symphony.

Speaking of Mullen, do you recall that I said that he threw his whole body into the part of "Archie". Check out the photo below. I rest my case.

I believe this photo was taken during an actual broadcast. I can't believe that the NBC Publicity people would have staged it with the actor in the foreground blocking my face. (Or did they?) The gentleman in soft focus in the foreground (obviously on his way to another microphone to deliver his lines), was a great character actor named Floyd Buckley. Floyd was an oldtimer who had been in show business for many years. He appeared in about 11 films during the period 1914 to 1920. I believe he was born in 1874, which means that when this photo was taken in1945, he was a pretty spry 71 years old. Why shouldn't he be? That's my age. ☺

I don't remember what part he was playing on this particular day, but I do recall that he was another of my favorites to work with. The reason...he was the voice of "Popeye" when Wheatina sponsored that radio program, and he would do that great voice for me whenever I asked. Floyd also lived out my way on Long Island, so whenever he was booked on the show we would often take the same train home together. He was filled with all sorts of entertaining stories and the trip passed quickly.

Those early programs were broadcast from NBC's studio 3B until we developed a sizable fan base for the show. Then, when the listenership increased to a sizable amount, NBC started to promote the fact that tickets would soon be available if anyone wanted to attend a live broadcast. When enough ticket requests justified it, the show then moved to the much larger Studio 6A, which could accommodate a few hundred people every Saturday.

That's when Charlie and I really cut loose. It's fun to play comedy in front of a live audience. We soon learned when to anticipate the laughs from the studio audience, and made sure we didn't try and talk over them. The show biz term was "Don't step on a laugh". But that required split second timing. One had to let the laugh die down a bit so our next line could be heard. However, the audience reaction was slow sometimes, and the joke took a second to sink in. In those instances, we were admonished by the director to be sure to "wait for the laugh". God forbid the laugh never came. Then we'd be stuck with what we called "dead air". That's why I say it required a certain instinct, and split second timing. I was fortunate I guess, because I learned all that during my years of stage experience.

But Charlie and I were not above "milking" the laughs by using exaggerated facial expressions and body lanquage. (It was shameful sometimes.) But we were encouraged to do it. It made the program sound like the audience was having way too much fun, and the ticket requests kept pouring in from the youngsters that made up our fan base.

But there were two problems associated with studio audience laughter. I have frequently been asked the question by people in the OTR Hobby, (those who collect tapes of those old shows)… *"How come we hear laughter, but the line wasn't all that funny?"*

I plead guilty. It's because we were probably doing something "physical" up there on the stage, and we engaged in what we called "sight gags" rather than meaningful funny dialogue. An example might be as follows. If the script called for "Archie " to take some foul tasting medicine for a cold or tummy ache, that in itself is not funny. But if you can imagine the grimace and god awful face he put on, the kids would squeal with delight. Simply think of any situation, like Archie and Jughead shivering from the cold, and you would see us do the "St. Vitus Dance" until we milked the laughter dry.

The great Radio Comedian Fred Allen once commented, something to the effect, *"that studio audiences ruined radio"*. If you stop and think about it, he was probably right. (I don't mean that it killed radio... TV did that.) But studio laughter, or a live audience reaction, could sometimes intrude on the concentration of the listener at home. But radio script writers often fell into the trap and began focusing on getting a live audience reaction. Consequently the style of material, (or the gag) changed . I think that's what Mr. Allen meant.

Based on the pencil I'm holding in my hand, I now realize that the previous picture (and this one) were taken during a rehearsal. We had long ago marked our scripts to highlight our lines of dialogue, but the pencil was kept handy to make cuts, (or notes), that the director might give us. If you look close, that's the "Archie" program's writer Carl Jampel on the left in the control room, and to the right, one of our earlier directors, Garnet Garrison. Notice that Garnet is looking down at his script, but he also had a stop watch going. Directors usually noted the cumulative time at the bottom of every page. Our audio engineer is hidden from view, just to the left of the director, and is intent on watching the meters on his control panel. (Either that, or he was an escaped felon who momentarily left the control room because he didn't want his picture taken.) ☺

I mentioned earlier that there were two problems connected with live audience laughter. The final one was "timing" of the program by the director. Since radio programs had to fit within a designated time period, directors used a stop watch to time rehearsals, and more critically, the dress rehearsal. With a comedy show, he had to anticipate where the audience might laugh, and factor that into the overall running time. If he estimated or guessed wrong, and the show was running long (hopefully, due to long laughs), or short, (darn), then we would get all sorts of hand signals from him when we got to the final few pages of the script.

If we were running long, he's point a finger in the general direction of the actors in the scene, and make quick circles with it. That simply meant, "speed up the delivery of the lines slightly". When we got back on schedule, (based on the timing notations on his script), he'd let us know we could go back to our normal paced delivery by touching that same pointed finger to the tip of his nose. (Simply meaning, "your right on time, or right on the nose".) If the program was running too short (perhaps because we had a "dead" audience that didn't laugh as much as he had anticipated), he would hold up two hands , fingers touching, then slowly pull them

198

away from each other. That was the "stretch" or " slow down" signal. To an actor, that was tougher. Sometimes and ad lib might help, but usually, just a more deliberate delivery of the line.

In many of the radio programs I worked on, really savvy directors might have planned ahead, and during rehearsals, indicated some dialogue as "optional cuts", and we would mark the script accordingly. That way, if the show was running far too long, (and he realized it early on), the Director would make it known to the performers, (in a variety of ways) that we were to make the optional cuts, and proceed to scratch the lines out of our scripts. If we were busy on mike, and paying close attention to our scripts, he might signal to another performer who was not in the scene, and they would then approach us an let us know by pantomime, (or whisper in our ear) that the optional cut should be made.

I recall that Garnet Garrison took over as director of the show shortly after we began the series. For some reason, he didn't stay at the helm too long, and another director, Ed King, took over. I'm not too familiar with Garnet's other program credits, but as with so many other people I worked with in those early days, fate decreed that he and I would hook up again during my own directing career, but far from the New York scene.

Garnet Garrison left NBC in the early days of TV to accept the position as head of the newly formed Radio/TV department at the University of Michigan. Early in my own TV production career, (following college), I took a job with a local TV station in Michigan to hone my craft, and apply what I learned in school. Somehow, Garnet Garrison discovered that I was in the area, and would invite me down to his University as a guest lecturer for those students in the TV production classes. That was fun.

199

But there is an even more significant connection with my later career in TV production because of working with Ed King when he briefly directed our show. Ed amassed quite a few credits in radio, (as well as early live TV). Some of the radio shows he directed were "The Adventures of Frank Merriwell", "Believe it or Not", "The Chase", "David Harum", "Dimension X", "Just Plain Bill", "The New Theatre" and "A Tree Grows in Brooklyn", etc.

Ed only directed the Archie show for a brief time, but I worked with him on other programs, and he was a most friendly and approachable guy. When I returned to NBC (and the "Archie" show) after my brief Air Force career, I bumped into Ed, and asked for a few minutes of his time. He readily agreed. I told him I was looking for some advice, and I asked him what he thought about the idea of my making the transition from actor to director. He responded immediately, saying something to the effect that *"based on my years as an actor, I could probably make the transition easily. Basically, all I needed to do was learn the "stopwatch".* That was Ed's way of saying the "technical" side of the business.

I took his advice, went to school to learn all that stuff, and the rest is history. (But as I said earlier…that's a whole'nuther book!) Ironically, as it turned out, the college I attended (Hofstra) did not offer TV Production courses. I had to go to Columbia University at night to learn that new medium, and transfer the credits to Hofstra. Guess who my Professor was in two of those TV Production courses? Ed King of course.

I now thank him publicly, (and posthumously) for his earlier advice and encouragement, not to mention getting straight "A's" in the courses he taught. It's amazing how contacts made early in life can have a profound effect on a career in this business.

Now...getting back to those fun years. Well, when I say fun, you have to realize that we were reaching the end of a devastating World War in 1945. But Charlie and I, as teenagers, were fairly insulated from any effect that it had on our day to day lives.

Until one day, Charlie got a message from Uncle Sam. He had just turned 18, and his services were requested in another "theatre". (They called the Pacific and European combat areas "Theatres of War" for some dumb reason.)

Although the war was already over in Europe, Charlie, along with thousands of other young men, were needed as replacements for the veterans who had accumulated enough "points" and were eligible to return home. Besides, the Army still needed lots of fresh troops to fill the ranks of the occupation forces in the conquered European war zones .

Speaking of our Victory in Europe, I vividly recall an experience that Charlie and I shared one evening. Both of us had been invited to dinner one night at the apartment of an older actor named Bill Griffith. Bill was practically a regular member of the "Archie" cast, playing a variety of parts when other characters were needed for the story lines. Like the local druggist, or cab driver, or salesperson, etc. Bill had great flexibility, so he could fit into many vocal guises. And I believe he was good friends with the then current Director, Charlie Urquhart. As I said earlier, when you were liked by a director, and you could handle the role, you were called often.

I mention this dinner invitation solely to indicate that cast members also had a social life of sorts outside the studio, particularly when it was a long term association, and a long running show.

I'll cover some of those social events as this tale unfolds. But it was not unusual that Bill Griffiths, who was probably twice our age, would invite two teenage cut-ups to a home cooked meal. But such was the camaraderie that existed between cast members.

I recall this event so vividly not because the food was so good, but because during dinner, the radio program that we were listening to was interrupted with a news bulletin. Germany had surrendered. It was VE day. New York city erupted with the news. The three of us quickly finished dinner and went out into the streets, as did the rest of the denizens of the apartment buildings throughout the entire city. It was a scene of such spontaneous jubilation that it will be forever etched in my memory. I recall Bill Griffith lived uptown in the low 70's, off 7th Ave. The three of us proceeded to walk all 30 blocks down to Times Square (42nd street), The joy, jubilation, and frenzy, increased in intensity the closer we got to Times Square. Vehicular traffic was nonexistent. Cars and cabs couldn't possibly have moved with the hordes of people dancing and walking in the middle of the streets, all heading for Times Square, from all points of the compass. Cars and cab drivers contented themselves with a continuous honking of horns, or simply leaving their vehicles along the side streets and joined the marching throng. An evening I shall never forget.

Now that I think of it, the dinner that Bill Griffith hosted that evening might well have been a going away party for Charlie before he had to report to the Army for basic training.

One other event that I remember sharing with Charlie was to eyewitness the aftermath of a tragic event in NYC. While we were in the middle of an "Archie" show being broadcast on Saturday morning, July 28, 1945, we were unaware that the show was interrupted with a news bulletin which announced that an Army B-25 bomber, lost in the fog, crashed into the side of the Empire State Building. We were informed of that fact immediately after we got off the air, and since the fog had lifted, we walked a few blocks and were able to see the gaping hole with smoke still billowing from it. It was a strange feeling to observe the damage and hear about the loss of life. I couldn't conceive of something so horrible. But I was to learn differently after 9/11.

Now, getting back to Charlie's departure from the show. As the time drew closer and closer, NBC was frantically scurrying around trying to find someone to replace him before he had to leave. But before I get to that, I might as well finish up with the future trials, tribulations and triumphs of one Charles Harold Mullen.

It seems the United States Army didn't always mess up in assigning new recruits to posts or job functions that they were ill equipped to handle. Thankfully, Charlie was not destined to be a "grunt" assigned to the Infantry. Some bright personnel officer paid some note to Charlie's civilian career, and he was put into Special Services, and served out the rest of his enlistment in the Armed Forces Radio detachment out there in sunny Los Angeles. It was a dirty job, but somebody had to do it.

Charlie eventually rose to the rank of Technical Sergeant, and when his enlistment was up, came back to the welcoming throngs of New Yorkers who appreciated his defending them in that distant and dangerous outpost. ☺

However, during his absence, his replacement in the part of "Archie" was firmly entrenched in the role, and well liked by everyone at NBC, including his fellow cast members, not to mention our then sponsor, the Swifts Meat Packing company.

That put NBC in a bit of a bind. In theory, all returning servicemen were supposed to be given their civilian jobs back after discharge. After all, it was only fair that they should be given that sort of consideration after the sacrifices they made. (No, I'm not being sarcastic about Charlie's contribution to the war effort.) Charlie was lucky. He could just as easily have been put in harms way were it not for some Army officer with brains who put a round peg in a round hole.

According to Charlie's biography "The Last Renaissance Man", published in 2001, Charlie stated that it was his good friend, noted comedic actor, Arnold Stang, who urged Charlie to stand up for his rights as a returning serviceman and try to get his job back.

It was a sticky situation, and NBC easily solved it. First, they decided they needed to continue with the status quo and not make any changes in the cast. But, they agreed to pay Charlie Mullen the same talent fee that his replacement (another ex- serviceman) was being paid for playing "Archie", and everyone was happy. Charlie was supposed to work the talent fees off by appearing on other programs. But if they didn't have a part for him in any given week, he still got paid. Some of those appearances were on "Eternal Light" for Frank Papp, and "Believe it or Not" for Ed King.

In the meantime, Charlie got married to a lovely young lady named Gloria, and desirous of starting a family, and realizing the uncertainty of the acting profession, decided he better find other work to supplement his income whenever acting assignments became few and far between.

I'm condensing things a bit, but in the beginning of 1950, Charlie also took a job as a route salesman selling Lucky Strike cigarettes in Brooklyn for the American Tobacco Company. He could pretty much set his own hours to make the rounds, and still be available for some radio work. He kept his hand in the acting profession, and in 1951, made the transition to TV performing, and played the part of "Dexter" in "Kiss and Tell".

But Charlie's success as a salesman for the American Tobacco only succeeded in his gaining a great deal of recognition within that company, and he kept getting promoted (with greater responsibilities), and eventually became the District Sales Manager. However, it didn't end there. But it sure meant he couldn't devote time to both occupations, so he had to give up his first love, performing.

WOULD YOU BELIEVE THAT MY GOOD BUDDY, CHARLES HAROLD MULLEN, BECAUSE OF HIS PERSONALITY, DRIVE, TALENT AND AMBITION, EVENTUALLY BECAME CHAIRMAN OF THE BOARD OF THAT FORTUNE 500 COMPANY, THE AMERICAN TOBACCO COMPANY?

Now, I ask you, is that a success story or what? See what can be accomplished when you set your mind to it? Wow! Was I ever impressed. And I don't want to hear any "Tsk! Tsk! from anybody out there because Charlie's success was with a company that sold an no-no product to the unsuspecting masses. Let's just consider that, back then, all the ills of cigarette smoking were not as well documented as they are today. Case closed.

Now, are you ready? Brace yourself. A goodly portion of the rest of this book will be devoted to another sterling individual, an extremely talented actor, handsome man about town, good buddy, and one destined for stardom, who eventually took over the part of Archie. (He paid me to say that.)

Here's the way it happened. During Charlie's final weeks on the show, NBC was auditioning like mad to find a replacement that could handle the part as well as Charlie did. They wanted to preserve the same quality that he brought to the character, and that wasn't easy. That quest kept me busy after the end of each Saturday broadcast. Following the show, I'd have to hang around the studio to read opposite the candidates when they came in to audition for the role.

One fine day, into studio 6A, walks this handsome Army Air Force officer, wearing his dress pinks. As you can imagine, because of my interest in the military back then, I almost snapped to attention. He explained to the director that he was visiting a friend on the second floor who told him they were holding open auditions for "Archie", and would there be an opportunity for him to read for the part. Now, who could say no to one of our returning "heros"?

Actually, I jokingly accused him later on that he wore his uniform to the audition that day just to evoke sympathy and influence the casting decision based on patriotic zeal and the love affair the county had for our returning G.I.'s.

That was my first encounter with the infamous Lt. Bobby Hastings. And I'm thrilled that it was not destined to be my last.

Bobby got the part because I told the director that I'd work with the kid a bit and teach him everything I knew. (Just kidding, folks.) But you must understand something. After working with him over the following 7 or 8 years, this is one of the rare occasions that I can get a word in edgewise concerning him, and he can't get back at me unless he writes his own book. Now I ask you. Does this look like someone you'd trust to be a Bombardier-Navigator of a very expensive B-29 bomber?

But we were not to be graced with Mr. Hasting's presence immediately following Charlie Mullen's last appearance as "Archie" on the program. It seems that there was to be a two week delay before Bob Hastings became a civilian again, and was available to take over the role. He had to finish up his final mustering- out- of- service routine and obtain his Honorable Discharge.

 A little know fact. The part of "Archie" was then played for that interim two week period by another young journeyman actor named Jimmy Dobson. But that wasn't the only time he appeared on our program.

 Jimmy was also hired to play other teenagers every so often, but was often used in the role of "Archie's" principal teenage antagonist "Reggie Mantle".

Jimmy Dobson eventually moved to the West Coast to appear in a few minor roles in Motion Pictures during the period 1947-51. However, they were "uncredited" roles in films titled "Boomerang", "They Live By Night" and "On Moonlight Bay". I also remember seeing him in a small part in a War movie whose title I forget. He did a little television work, with an appearance on "Sergeant Preston of the Yukon" in 1955, but eventually drifted out of the business. I heard that Jimmy passed away in 1964, at a much too early age.

Now we focus on the gentleman who is the most closely identified with playing "Archie" because of his many years in the role…and quite possibly, because he looked a lot like the comic book character.

Not so much around the nose and eyes perhaps, or the eyebrows for that matter. And no discernible freckles to be sure. But the mouth, as you can see, is right on target.

Bobby was about 5 years older than I was at the time, but lately, he claims to be many years my junior. But back then, (thankfully), he never treated me like some wet behind the ears kid, and he could act as silly as the rest of us when we were in character. (But then again, sometimes "out" of character as well.) I think that's partly due to the fact that he will never grow up, and never ages. Despite being frozen in time. He is now a proud father and grandfather many times over. (He's probably even a Great Grandfather by now.) Whenever I see him lately, I swear he keeps getting face lifts. No one that old should look that young. But his lovely and charming wife, Joan, swears that he's not a retouched individual, or a younger looking clone.

One of the nicest things that I can say about Bob is that he was smart enough to marry Joan Rice, his childhood sweetheart, who he met when they both performed as young singers on the NBC Kids show, "Coast to Coast on a Bus".

That's not at all surprising, since Bob began his early show business career as a child singer around 9 years of age. His first radio appearances were on NY newspaper columnist Nick Kenny's "The Daily Mirror Gang". That led to work singing on two network kid's shows, the aforementioned "Coast to Coast on a Bus", and a show called "Our Barn". During that period, some NY Ad Agency dude heard him sing, and he was booked for a few appearances on "The National Barn Dance".

I know for certain that at age 18, when Bob went into the military, he was still pretending to be a young kid singing on "Coast to Coast on a Bus". He was a tenor, and you know how tough it is to pinpoint their ages.

As for some of the dramatic radio credits he accumulated, I'm not sure which ones were prior, post or simultaneous with his 7/8 years as "Archie", but they included "Pretty Kitty Kelly", "Hilltop House", "This is Nora Drake", " The Sea Hound", "Cavalcade of America", and "Dimension X", to name a few.

As with many radio performers, Bob made the transition into Television a good 4 years before the "Archie" show went off the air. But the big difference between Bob (and so many of the other radio actors of that period), was that he parlayed his talent into a very long and successful career in films and TV, particularly after his move to the West Coast, where many more TV programs originated.

I believe his bio indicates that the first live TV show he did (back in 1949) was on "Captain Video" which originated from NY. Wasn't that the program that his younger brother Donald co-starred on? Hmmm? I'd call that reverse nepotism. Some people will do anything to get ahead, including riding on your kid brother's coat-tails. ☺

Do you see the family resemblance? I tried to get Bob to send me a recent picture (like his brother Donald did) so you could see what I mean. But apparently, Bob's photo retoucher was out of town, and he told me to use the one I already had.

OK. Time to get serious. Bob had a great deal of talent, and did a great deal of work over many years in Show Business. As a matter of fact, he was still doing the voice of "Commissioner Jim Gordan" on the "Batman" animated series as recently as 2001, (a part he first began playing in 1992.) Another animated show that used his voice between 1966/69 was "The Superman" series, playing "Superboy/Clark Kent" . (Wonder of wonders, his voice must have finally changed in 1970.)

But Bobby was more than just a voice. Obviously when you consider the vast amount of on-camera roles he played.

I won't list them all. (He's not paying me enough) . ☺

However, I'd have to believe that his most recognizable role on TV was as "Lt. Carpenter" on the long running and popular series "McHales Navy". In case you have a short memory, (and it's not still in syndication on your local station), he played the suck-up aide and "yes man" to Captain Binghamton, who was always being driven crazy by McHale and his wild bunch. Particularly by that funny man Tim Conway. Bobby parlayed that notoriety into cutting a record album of old favorites, titled "Bob Hastings sings for the Family". (What? Not singing for the bucks?) You can't fool me.

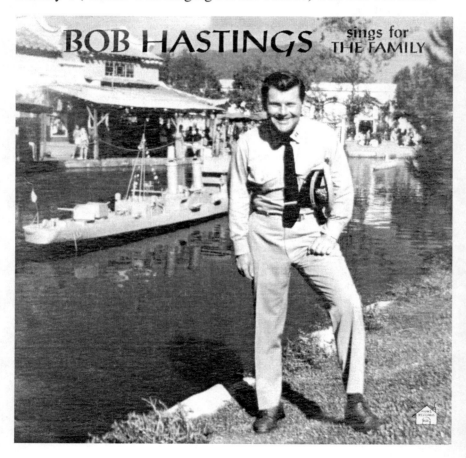

BOB HASTINGS sings for THE FAMILY

But Bob became a big favorite on the Universal lot, and was even hired to be one of the celebrities that would make appearances at the Universal Studios tourist attraction, meeting and greeting the people he would encounter there. (Much like Micky Mouse does at Disneyland.) Hey, promotion is an all important part of Show Business. Bob was so popular at this publicity activity for Universal, he became known as the "Mayor" of the Universal Studio tour.

I just remembered something that Bob told me a few years ago about his audition for the part of "Lt. Carpenter" on "McHales Navy". It seems the producer (or director) had been a big fan of the "Archie Andrews" radio show many years earlier. In our business, things like that often tipped the scales when casting decisions were made. (Not to mention that his talent was probably heads and shoulders above the competition, right?)

Bob's popularity with the "brass" at Universal probably helped when he was selected to co-star with the lovely Eileen Wesson in the 1967 film "Did You Hear The One About The Traveling Saleslady?"

Since I'm running out of pictures of Bob from his later acting days, (and I'm trying to hold the page count of this book to about 320), let me just finish up by saying he did a ton of work out there in "Tinsel Town".

I mean we're talking about appearances on very popular shows like "Green Acres", " Adam-12". "I Dream of Jeannie", Hogan's Heros", "Petticoat Junction" , "Ben Casey", "The Untouchables", "Real McCoys", "Rockford Files", "The Waltons"… Phew! The list goes on and on and on.

Will someone please remind me to treat him with more respect the next time I see him? Honestly folks, until I downloaded all his credits from the internet, I never realized what a busy actor he had been ever since our early "Archie" days together. Not that we didn't stay in touch over the years. But I was engrossed with my own TV Directing career back in NY and wasn't paying too much attention to what was happening out on the West Coast.

One of the nicest things I can say about the guy was that he never let success go to his head. Whenever we met later on in life, I didn't have to hear how successful he had become. He took it all in stride, and didn't become afflicted with the "Smell me, I'm a Star", Hollywood nonsense. But that modesty was usually the case with most of the performers who had their start in radio. They treated their acting craft in a more matter of fact way, and didn't get swelled heads when they became TV celebrities. It was all in a days work as far as they were concerned

Oh, I almost forgot to mention his performing on another incredibly popular TV show. "All in the Family". He did a bit in the recurring role of "Kelsey the Bartender" for about 5 years.

I'm sure I probably left out mentioning a show he did that he was particularly proud of, and if that's the case, I beg his forgiveness. But as they say, "Oh Well...That's Show Biz".

I had now planned to tell you folks about another significant cast change in the "Archie" show that took place shortly after Bobby joined us, but I just realized this "Scene" (chapter) is running long. I didn't expect to spend so much time talking about Hastings. They say "brevity is the soul of wit". Do I hear Bob Hastings now saying *"See. I always thought he was witless"*.

Act 3

Scene 2

(Music) "Somewhere Over the Rainbow, Blue Birds Fly"

(Establish music, then fade under)

(CUE NARRATION)

To paraphrase the theme music , it should be "Seagulls Fly" over the rainbow. Back in those glory days of broadcasting, the NBC studios were housed in the lower floors of a huge skyscraper then known as the RCA Building. The top floor was home to the Rainbow Room, a restaurant with an incredible view. (And seagulls did fly that high, going from the East River over to New York Harbor.) Radio actors went there mostly for "power lunches" and special occasions. A terrible pun would be to say that my going there at that stage in my life "was the high point of my career". Most working actors had lunch at Hurley's, or the restaurant adjacent to the skating rink, or the coffee shop on the lower level.

Anyway, that intro brings us back to NBC and the early days of the "Archie" program. As you learned 15 pages ago, Bob Hastings had just joined our happy little group. Shortly after his arrival, Doris Grundy (our first "Betty") announced she had to leave the show, and was going off to California. Hmmmm? Did Bobby scare her?

217

The next thing we knew, a very pretty young blonde lady shows up in the studio and was introduced to us (by our then director, Charlie Urquhart), as our new "Betty". From that moment on, Rosemary Rice became a very most welcome addition to

the cast, and remained in that role until the very end
She played "Betty" to perfection. Rosemary was
the epitome of the "Girl Next Door" type. And her
portrayal of the sweet, unassuming, Betty was a
wonderful counterpoint to the way Gloria Mann
played the "vixen" and self centered "Veronica".

Despite the fact that Rosemary Rice had started in "glamour-
ous" show business as a child, she was as unaffected and as sweet
as the role she played. And I hasten to add, remains that way to this
very day. I thoroughly enjoyed working with her, as did the rest of
the cast. But I do recall Bobby and I would sometimes tease her
because she was just a trifle gullible (or was it "trusting"?). But
we never did it maliciously. We just knew which buttons to push
just to get a reaction out of her. But she soon realized it was done
good naturedly and was able to handle her own.

I mentioned Rosemary started in the business as a youngster.
Her career path was similar to mine. Her first professional appearance was on Broadway at age 13. She played the character of
"Fluffy" in the hit play "Junior Miss". She later appeared in another stage hit, playing "Miriam" in "Dear Ruth". That play ran for
two years, and it was her performance in "Dear Ruth" that led to
her landing the role of "Betty" on "Archie Andrews". Not to
mention many other radio shows.

I love the story that Rosemary tells how that all came about. It
seems that the cast members of "Dear Ruth" realizing that the play
was coming towards the end of it's run, were concerning themselves with finding other work. So Rosemary, (18 years old by
then), very cleverly hatched the following scheme. She arranged to
buy numerous tickets to her play, and sent them in pairs (as gifts)

to many of the influential radio producers and directors of that period. A nice note was included that introduced herself, while explaining that she hoped they would attend, enjoy the show, and after seeing her performance, perhaps consider her for other work.

One fateful evening, following her performance, there came a knock at her dressing room door. When she opened it, there was this very tall & lanky guy standing there who introduced himself as Charlie Urquhart, director of the "Archie Andrews" radio program. He explained that he was in the process of auditioning young ladies as a replacement for the part of "Betty", and informed Rosemary that he thought she would be perfect in that role. Say what you will about Charlie Urquhart (and I will a little later on) he certainly was a good judge of talent. I know that for a fact, because he once told me that I was perfect in the part of "Jughead".
(You guys know when I'm kidding around, right?)

At any rate, the lovely and gracious Rosemary Rice occupies a special niche in my heart to this day. And like my other dear friend Roberto Hastings, she accomplished a great deal during her multi faceted (and ongoing) career.

Would you believe she was the winner of 3 "Clio" awards" (given for excellence in TV commercials), a "Grammy" (for music), the "Pulitzer Prize" (literature), 3 "Peabody Awards" (broadcasting) and an "EMMY" for TV. And I'm happy to report that none of that has gone to her head. She is still as sweet and charming as she was the day I first met her many long years ago.

Since I had trouble recounting all of Mr. Hastings credits, (time and space limitations) I'll have to condense Rosemary's as well.

I'd have to say, (in my opinion), Rosemary's most memorable role was playing "Katrin" in the long running TV series, "I Remember Mama". (Aside from playing "Betty" on "Archie" of course). ☺ Adorable, right? And as charming as she was good looking.

Rosemary played on that TV program for 8 long years.

In addition to Rosemary, the cast featured Peggy Wood as "Mama", Judson Laire as "Papa", my child acting buddy, Dick Van Patten, as Rosie's brother "Nels", and Robin Morgan as the younger sister "Dagmar".

"Mama", (as it was affectionately dubbed by insiders in the business) first came to the public's attention as a stage play. Then, it was adapted for Radio as a one shot on "The Cavalcade of America" radio program, and starred that well known actress of the period, Irene Dunne. But guess who played Katrin? None other than our Rosie. Consequently, when they were casting for someone to play that role in the TV series, (back in mid 1949) Rosemary was the ideal choice. That meant that Rosemary had two running parts. One on radio, playing "Betty" in our show, and "Katrin" on TV. Actors love to be kept busy.

Rosemary amassed quite a few stage credits before all this TV work. In addition to the previously mentioned stage roles, she was also in "Franklin Street", "Brief Holiday", "Love on Leave" , "Pick up Girl", "The Bees and the Flowers", etc.

Some of her radio work consisted of appearances on "Studio One", "Let's Pretend" , "Cavalcade of America", "My True Story", CBS Mystery Theatre", "When a Girl Marries", "Young Dr. Malone", "NBC Playhouse", and of course, the biggie (in my jaded opinion), "The Adventures of Archie Andrews".

Other TV credits included appearances on daytime "soaps" such as "Edge of Night", "Search for Tomorrow", "One life to Live", "As the World Turns", and some major prime-time dramatic shows, like "Playhouse 90", and numerous appearances on "Kraft Television Theatre". Not to mention, a ton of TV commercials.

Throughout her life, Rosemary had other fish to fry. She was also extremely interested in writing and performing children's books and record albums. She did 10 such albums for Columbia, and 6 for RCA, as well as a number of children's "Books on Tape". Consequently, when not performing, she achieved success and conquered the "Children's Educational Entertainment" medium.

I love that preceding photo of Rosemary . The "Doris Day" type for sure. And I was in love with the "Doris Day" type in my early teenage years. Until I discovered Sophia Loren. But my platonic affection for Rosie never wavered, even when "Sophia" beckoned down at me from the big screen. ☺

As you will soon learn, the "Archie" cast was not to maintain its status quo for very long. Particularly when it came to the role of Archie's Dad, "Mr. Fred Andrews". Over the years, we had at least 5 different cast changes after Vinton Hayworth left. Vinton was followed by another neat guy named Ian Martin. I tried to find a picture of Ian, but no luck. His other radio credits included a long running part on "Big Sister", and appearances on "The CBS radio Mystery Theatre", "The Chase", "Crime Fighters", "Now Hear This", and "The Right to Happiness". Ian perhaps played the role of "Mr. Andrews" for about a year, and left to honor other commitments.

Ian was also a stage performer. I recall he was one of the principal characters in the hit Broadway musical "Finnian's Rainbow". He ultimately gained quite a reputation as a writer, doing scripts for "CBS's Adventure Theatre". In later years, he kept very busy writing scripts for TV Soaps.

You're not going to believe this. We also had a <u>very famous</u> radio personality play the part for about two weeks. None other than the very popular and busy performer, Raymond Edward Johnson. All the died-in-the-wool OTR fans know him as the scary host of "The Inner Sanctum".

225

I seem to recall Ray stepping into the role of "Fred Andrews" on some sort of emergency basis, perhaps an illness. Or maybe it was just Raymond helping out on a temporary stop-gap measure while the director looked for someone to play the role full-time.

Raymond Johnson was one of the biggest names in radio, and also one of the nicest and most personable guys to work with. His many credits included "Arch Oblers Plays", "A Brave Tomorrow", "Calvacade of Tomorrow", "Cloak and Dagger", "Crime Fighters", "Dimension X", "Don Winslow of the Navy", "Famous Jury Trials", "Gang Busters", "The Guiding Light", and of course, his most famous role on "Inner Sanctum" (also played at one point by my friend, Paul McGrath). I can still hear them do the program's opening. First came the squeaking door sound effect...then, in the most sinister voice, *"Welcome...This is Raymond, your host"*. Brrr! It brought chills to my teenage soul, and no doubt, to millions of other listeners who were hooked on that really scary program.

Following Ray's temporary run in our cast, we were joined by a man who was to play the role for many years, right on up to the program's finale. Except for a strange interlude of 13 weeks which I'll mention shortly. But first, I have to give Arthur Kohl his due for playing the part of "Mr. Andrews" so well, and for so long. We all definitely enjoyed our long  association with the man. (Sorry that I couldn't find a more flattering picture of him among my stuff.)

Arthur may have been in his late 50's early 60's when he started playing "Mr. Andrews", but after working with Bobby and me for so long (6 or 7 years), he probably aged 20 more.

Some of his other radio credits included roles on "Author's Playhouse", "Bachelor's Children", "Right to Happiness", and TWICE as Archie's dad. That strange turn of events came about this way.

After being sponsored by "Swifts Premium Franks" for about a year, there was a dry spell as far as sponsors went, and we were sustaining again for quite some time. The NBC sales staff went at it hot and heavy to find someone else to bankroll the program. Somehow or other, a deal was worked out with the "Kraft Foods" ad agency, who were looking for a 13 week summer replacement for their Wednesday night prime time hit show, "The Great Gildersleeve".

But it seems that NBC Program executives in NY had to make a concession. One of the better known performers on the West Coast must have had a friend in high places at the ad agency in Los Angeles. I'm talking about none other than Arthur Q. Bryan who played the part of "Doc Gamble" on "Fibber McGee and Molly". It's quite possible that Bryan, (even more famous for doing the voice of "Elmer Fudd" in all the "Bugs Bunny" cartoons) was added to the cast as an inducement to get Kraft to sponsor the program. Perhaps it was hoped his celebrity status and "name value" might possibly carry over and draw a bigger audience in that time slot.

Nobody said life was fair, right. Arthur Kohl was told his services would not be needed when the show went to Wednesday nights. (Actually, Bob and I thought it was a dirty deal for Arthur Kohl.) But I'm happy to relate that Arthur K. came back on the program after that 13 weeks for "Kraft", and Arthur Q. went back to LA.

Arthur Q. Bryan was an interesting character, and seemed like a decent enough guy. I mean, you have to give him credit. His "Elmer Fudd" voice was a classic. Out in L.A., he also worked on "The Charlotte Greenwood Show", "Blondie", "The Al Pearce Show", and had a great run on "Fibber McGee and Molly". His bio also includes working on the "Ethel Merman Show". Hmm!. I also appeared on that show, but it originated in New York. I wonder if Arthur Q. also did that show while he was back East playing on "Archie" with us that one summer?

Moving on. I think we had as many directors who worked on the show as we did actors who played "Mr. Andrews". But most of the changes occurred in the first few years. I mentioned Tony Leader, Garnett Garrison, and Ed King. I think we even had Frank Papp for a brief period.

Frank was an extremely dapper looking gent, with slick black hair, and a trim mustache. He looked like a smaller version of Clark Gable. Some of the other shows he was responsible for were "Right to Happiness", "Eternal Light", and "Words at War". Frank tried to make the transition to TV, and directed a few of the early live TV shows, but unfortunately, he didn't stay on top of the technical changes and advances in the business, and confided to me years later that he didn't know the first thing about Videotape. The fast changing technical aspects of the business passed him by.

I think the next director to follow Frank Papp was a truly

certifiable character named Charlie Urquhart. (Remember, I mentioned him earlier as the guy that cast Rosemary Rice in the part of "Betty".)

Charlie was unique. He was very tall, gaunt, had a horse face, and looked a lot like the famous Motion Picture director John Houston in his younger days. Charlie also "snorted" like a horse when he laughed, which he did often. He also dressed a bit flamboyantly, wore a floppy fedora, loud patterned vests, and carried a cane. (I think the cane was for affect.). Charlie once told me his career began with the circus. Actually, it probably was with a carnival, because he would have made a great sideshow "barker" or "pitchman". How he got into radio, I never found out. I think he did the show for a few years, and probably would have lasted much longer in the business were it not for a drinking problem. NBC canned him. I also heard that Charlie may have been a little too interested in young boys. But all I know was that I liked the guy when he was our director, and these problems didn't surface until he had left the show.

The next and last guy to become our Director was also a delightful person. And very good at his job. Ken McGregor stayed with us for many years. He was a burly, barrel chested, mostly bald Scotsman who was married to the most beautiful woman I ever saw in my life. Some of Ken's other directorial assignments for NBC were "City Desk", "Mystery in the Air", "Pretty Kitty Kelly", "Show Boat", "When a Girl Marries", "Bob and Ray", "X Minus One", and others. Ken didn't make the transition into television, but not for any lack of expertise. Some years after our show went off the air, he was tragically killed in an automobile accident on his way to work one day. I think I speak for all the members of our cast, Ken was probably our favorite director.

I've written quite a bit about those performers and directors who had careers in TV following the demise of radio entertainment. But I think the directors had the toughest time doing it.

Keep in mind that live TV came along at the same time radio was at it's zenith. It began as a mild form of competition, an "upstart", a curiosity. Not too many directors knew what to do about it. The good radio directors were still busy working in that audio medium, and either didn't take the time to learn this new visual craft, or couldn't conceive of it quickly replacing radio. Not to mention their livelihood.

I can hear the advice I got from that other OTR director Ed King. *"You just need to learn the stop watch"*. If Ed King gave that sage advice to fellow director Frank Papp, it went unheeded. Frank didn't bother to learn the technical side of TV, and by then, it was too late. A whole new breed had been waiting in the wings for many years (within the radio environment itself), and when TV first came along, they jumped at the chance. While the established directors were still doing radio shows, these young kids immediately swelled the TV production ranks, for little or no money. The old guard didn't want to take a pay cut to do the new (and often esthetically crude "Live TV" stuff), and in many cases, were ill prepared to make the transition.

And where did this "new breed" come from? Right under the noses of the established radio directors. The were members of NBC's Guest Relations staff. They were called "Pages".

The NBC Guest Relation Pages were glorified ushers, floor receptionists, with a touch of crowd control (live audiences), and a poor excuse for some semblance of security to keep strangers from wandering around the halls of NBC. They wore nice tailored dark blue uniforms, with some gold braid, stiff white shirt, black tie, and polished black shoes. They served as security at the main entrance to the NBC elevators, and manned desks on each floor to assist people (even actors sometimes) as to which studio such and such a show was in. A daily log was printed up each day so that these members of the Page staff knew what was happening, and where. Their other responsibility was to herd the masses of studio audiences into elevators on the ground floor, and upon being disgorged after reaching the 6th or 8th floor, they reformed them into lines and ushered them into a particular studio.

To many people, it would have been considered a low paying, boring, and thankless job. Ah, but not to these kids. The majority of these young men (and a few women) dreamed of being in show business. And in this environment, they were as close as one could get to it, and they kept their eyes and ears open. They went out of their way to be nice to performers, directors, producers and management. They all believed that some day, they might get their big break, and that perhaps, someone that they befriended might help them get inside the charmed circle.

As I grew older over the lifespan of the show, I was about the same age that they were. I became very friendly with many of them. They treated me with respect, and good fellowship, and I treated them the same. Many of them worked the "Archie" show for years, and once they learned that I was a "regular guy", I enjoyed their confidence and learned firsthand about their hopes and aspirations.

When early live TV came to NBC, there was no one trained or available to fill all the jobs that opened up. But guess who jumped at the chance? They couldn't believe their good fortune. Some of my favorite buddies on the page staff went on to fame and fortune in the Television industry.

Jimmy Gains and Johnny Van became TV directors, and both did the "Today Show" during their careers.

Do you recognize this guy? None other than the famous TV Quiz show host, Gene Rayburn.

When Gene was a Page working our show, he was as affable and entertaining as he was in his later appearances on the "Boob Tube".

I was always proud of what my former friends had achieved.

There was one other Page, (drat, his name escapes me now) who went on to play small roles in quite a few movies. He and I had a unique relationship. He looked enough like me to be my brother (practically a twin). We'd get the biggest kick when fans of the show mistook him for "Jughead" when he was wearing civilian clothes.

But I suppose the Page who went all the way to the top was Roone Arledge. He started out at the bottom as an NBC Page, then into production in the early days of live TV, and eventually head of Sports for ABC-TV, and ultimately, President of that company.

What's that old bromide, being in the right place at the right time? I think you'll agree that being a member of the Guest Relations staff at NBC during the waning days of radio, (and the birth of TV), is a prime example of that.

The one female page that I got to know quite well was named Neil. She married one of our Sound Effects men, Sam Monroe.

Being friends with a few of the NBC pages came in very handy sometimes.

Psst! Danny..Put the good looking blonde in the first row.

I could always count on them to make sure any friends of mine, who happened to be attending a broadcast, got the VIP treatment..

Usually, the cast finished our dress rehearsals session about 30 to 20 minutes before airtime. We left the stage, which allowed the pages to get the audience up from downstairs and into their theatre style seats. In those instances, if I had special guests or friends attending, I'd generally go downstairs myself to meet them in the lobby, whisk them upstairs before the stampede, then into the studio before anyone else, and put them "Front Row Center". But if we were running late, I could count on the Pages to take care of those things for me.

I shamelessly admit to trying to impress whatever pretty young thing I was taken with at that moment in my life. But from age 14 to 23, I discovered young girls were very fickle, so I was in and out of teenage crushes on a regular basis. However, I did get engaged at age 18, but that was a disaster. The less I say about it the better.

But I wonder? They say "Sex" sells books. Dare I digress again at this point and bring up the pitfalls of a teenager with raging hormones? Oh what the hell! Fools rush in where angels fear to tread.

Being raised by an extremely strict Catholic zealot mother, I was taught that one did not have impure thoughts, or even consider any form of sexual contact unless one was married. Consequently, I was mentally "handcuffed" whenever I was dating a young girl. As aroused as I might have gotten while "petting", I couldn't possibly do anything about it for fear of committing a terrible crime (sin) against the opposite sex. I mean after all, they were all Virgins right? And in the image of the Virgin Mary, right? Boy, was I ever brainwashed by my mother.

But all that came to a screeching halt when I was about 17. Speaking of Virginity… That's when I lost mine. And because I was not the animal predator, or instigator, I had no guilts about it whatsoever. I was simply the hapless and totally helpless victim. (Yeah, sure! Right!) To make a long story short, (and to protect the names of the innocent) I'll just touch on the highlights.

There was a young divorced mother who lived near my hometown, who was also a member of a small country club that my family belonged to. Nothing pretentious. Just a few tennis courts, clubhouse, swimming pool and a few boat slips.

This lovely lady had a young son who was a huge fan of the "Archie Show", and I was the object of some intense hero worship from him. He was a nice enough youngster, very polite, and I didn't mind him hanging around me sometimes, while I was busy hanging around with the kids my own age.

One day, his bikini clad mother approached me, and profusely thanked me for being so kind to her son. Then she asked for a big favor. Would it be possible for me to get tickets to the program so she could bring her boy into New York to see the show? I of course replied, (being the gentleman that I was), *"Certainly... No problem, I'll be happy to get tickets for the two of you for the following week."*

They came to the show, I visited with them briefly after the broadcast, introduced the young boy to the rest of the cast, got him autographs, and thought that was the end of it.

About a week later, this same lovely bikini clad lady came up to me at the country club and was extremely effusive in her thanks for bringing such pleasure to her son. She went on and on about how much they both enjoyed the experience. So much so, that she insisted on taking me (along with her son) out for an early dinner some evening to adequately show her appreciation for my many kindnesses to him.

Being quite sophisticated for my age, I was always able to handle myself around adults, and was not the slightest taken back by the offer. I told her that it wasn't necessary to thank me, I enjoyed being helpful, etc. But… she was charmingly insistent. What the heck, she was pleasant and fun, the kid was nice, so I said *"Sure, why not?"* Then she said "How about tonight?" And I said *"Ok. But let me call home first and check with my Mother"*.

Hey, I was a dutiful son. It wasn't that I needed permission, I just had to let 'em know what social activities were being scheduled, and that I wouldn't be home for dinner.

But seeing as how I was dressed in tennis attire, it was not suitable for restaurant dining. I mentioned that to my "hostess", and said I'd need to go home and change first. She said *"No problem. I'll follow you home in my car, wait for you to change, and then we can go back to my place, (for her son and her to change) and head out from there, O.K?"*

That seemed like a reasonable plan to me. So we all gathered up our gear, and I hopped on my bike and rode home while she and her son followed in her car. What? Are you finding all this a bit ludicrous? Me too. ☺

We had a lovely dinner, and I was invited back to her apartment for an after dinner drink. (My Dad permitted me to have a cocktail or two from age 15 on.) Mild social drinking, moderation and responsibility, were taught to me at an early age. After all, in my career, I was with adults, in adult situations, from a very early age. (Except for one kind of adult activity up to that point in time.).

She told her son that it was past his bedtime, and packed him off to sleep. She phoned a neighbor and asked her to baby-sit him in a little while (so she could drive me home), but told the baby-sitter we were just finishing up our visit, and she'd get back to her.

Yeah!… About an hour later. All I know, we were sitting around sipping our drink and having a nice friendly chat. But it was in the dog days of summer, and very hot in the apartment. Suddenly, she comments on the heat, and apologizes that the air conditioning is woefully inadequate. She suggests I take my jacket off, and sit in a comfortable chair over by the window. She then asked if I could excuse her for a minute, saying *"I want to slip into something more comfortable"*.

BOING! It suddenly hit me. I had heard that line before in a lot of movies. Was this really happening to me? I started trembling all over while she was gone. My mind was racing. And when she came back into the room wearing nothing but a flimsy black negligee………

OK! Where did I leave off discussing all the cast changes that happened over the years that the Archie Show was on the air.

What?… Did I omit something about my discovery of my awakened desires? Oh yes. I had mentioned previously that I became engaged at age 18. (However, not to the lovely lady I just told you about.) No, this was to someone a lot more closer to my own age. Actually, the sister of a buddy of mine. But seeing how she was as interested in adult activities as my original mentor, I felt getting engaged was the honorable thing to do. After all, since my mother admonished me at an early age that one had to be married before engaging in sex, I reasoned that becoming "engaged" to be married was close enough, thereby eliminating any guilts.

237

But that relationship was not to last. All of this nonsense was taking place shortly after I entered the Air Force, and since I was about to be sent overseas, it made sense to me to get engaged. In addition to making things right in the guilt department, I also reasoned that a ring on her finger would keep her out of mischief while I was gone.

I had to return home on an emergency leave one day from my duties in a foreign land, (Family problems). It all happened so quickly, that I couldn't alert my fiancee that I'd be back home for a few days. After I addressed the family problems, I dashed right over to my girl's house to surprise her, and engage in some pre-marital (but legitimate) fun and games, but she had started without me. I found her in bed with some other guy.

You may ask, how did you feel about that? Did that turn you into a woman hater?

To which I respond. Yeah! Sort of! But, it didn't last long. I simply got in touch with my original "mentor", and drowned my sorrow in her arms. I guess I failed to mention that the divorcé and I had stayed friends (occasionally) over the years. (Until I got engaged of course). But after getting dis-engaged, one does need true friends to see them through rough times. ☺

To close this topic, let me just say that I finally got married (at age 25) to a very neat young lady, (following my graduation from college) , and eventually had two wonderful kids named Harold and Deborah Lee. But I had mentioned them much earlier. We had about 20 good years together. My fault that it wasn't longer.

NOW!   Can we go from the sublime to the equally sublime

and get back to my "professional" fun and games?

Which brings me to talk about the remaining two major cast changes that occurred on our show. One concerned having to temporarily replace yours truly as "Jughead", and the other, finding a replacement for Gloria Mann in the part of "Veronica". Since I believe in "ladies first", I'm only too happy to discuss the addition of another delightful female member to our cast. Meet Jane Webb.

Boy, I gotta tell you. Bob Hastings and I were blessed all those years, having such talented (and I hasten to add) gorgeous young ladies as co-stars.

To help me fill in the gaps regarding the time frame when all this occurred, I just got off the phone talking with the lovely Jane Webb, and between the two of us, we decided that precise dates weren't all that important to this narrative. Mostly because we don't remember. Heck, it was 50+ years ago, and our minds are cluttered with too many other dates and career activities.

But this much we do know. Gloria Mann, our "Archie" program's original "Veronica", left the show to get married to some guy named "Peter", and move out to Los Angeles. That was sometime between 1950/51. Jane then played "Veronica" for about 2 or 3 years until the show went off the air.

Jane, as with so many of the other performers in our cast, had achieved quite a bit of success in our business. However, with the exception of "Archie Andrews", Jane originally did a great deal of work on Network radio programs that originated out of Chicago, and later, on the West Coast.

Jane grew up in Chicago radio, playing "Jane", on that great kids show favorite, "Tom Mix & His Ralston Straightshooters". Her career includes over 25,000 broadcasts from Chicago, NY, and LA. She was a contract player on many of the "soaps" during that period, and was featured on "Lux Radio Theatre", "The Big Show", etc.

On the West Coast, during her 13 year affiliation with the production company, Filmation, she handled many of the female voices for the cartoons "Sabrina, the Teenage Witch", "Gilligan's Island", "The Brady Bunch", and, it shouldn't come as any surprise, she reprised her role as "Veronica" in the cartoon version of "Archie Andrews". I found out recently that Howard Morris, (the wonderful comedic "2nd Banana" on Sid Caesar's great TV show) did the voice of "Jughead" for that cartoon series.

I guess they didn't know how to reach me at the time. ☺

But I'm not sure I would have been interested anyway. I was too engrossed and happy doing my TV directing thing. Ooops, sorry. We were talking about Jane's accomplishments.

As far as motion pictures were concerned, she worked on "The Andromeda Strain", "Bonnie and Clyde", "Ghost Story" and "Terms of Endearment".

She even has something in common with her friend and acting buddy, Rosemary Rice. It seems Jane also worked on recording audio books for children, editing and narrating storytime favorites for the Audio Book company. She also added numerous commercials to her credits.

Jane retired in 1987. At that time, she was working as a staff announcer at KABC-TV in Los Angeles. I'm happy to state that Jane (and her husband, Jack Edwards), eventually moved to Arizona, (my current home state) and we keep threatening to get together, but they live way down South, and we're in the Northern part, so it's not all that easy.

We did have an opportunity of sorts about 7 years ago, when Bob Hastings, his wife Joan, Jane and Jack, all converged at my house. We had a great reunion talking about the good old days.

By the way, you might enjoy reading a note that Jane sent me. I had asked for her bio when I started writing this book. I think it serves to illustrate how modest and self effacing some of these marvelous performers are.

4/28/02

Hi Hal—
    Here's a resume of sorts. It didn't name the "soaps" — too many of 'em — but partial list:
    "The Bartons" "Guiding Light" (that was early chicago)
    "Lone Journey," "ma Perkins," "The Baxters," "That Brewster Boy", "Judy & Jane," "Aunt Mary."
    Also "First nighter" "Dr. Kildare", "Box 13,"
    oh, forget about it!!
            Best
            Jane

Incidentally, Jane's husband Jack was also in the business, as was Jack's brother Sam. (Jane's favorite Brother-in-Law, in case you haven't figured that out.) I see Sam Edwards a great deal more than I see Jane and jack. Sam was a heavy duty performer in Radio, and is a frequent guest at many of the Old Time Radio Conventions. But I have to share this with you. Of all the characters and voices that Jane's brother-in law played over his long career, a stellar performance had to be as the voice of "Thumper" the rabbit, in the classic Disney animated film, "Bambi".

Speaking of "deers", when I found out just a few years ago that Sam Edwards played "Thumper" (my childhood favorite character), he "endeared" himself to me no end. Gee, sometimes I hate myself for puns like that.

Ok. We are coming to the end of the "musical chairs" routine with the actors on the "Archie" show. It eventually became my turn The reason I needed to be replaced as "Jughead" was due to the fact that I was now over 18, had reached military age, and things were getting nasty in Korea.

Since I was now "draft age", I decided that I really wasn't interested in being drafted into the Army. I wanted something more glamorous, like the Air Corps. I knew that I couldn't be a pilot because I had not yet gone to college. So the warrior in me thought that the next best thing (as an enlisted man) would be to become an Aerial Gunner on a bomber. (Yeah! I was gung ho for sure.) And totally indoctrinated by all the war movies I grew up watching. And if you recall earlier in this book, I was always hooked on things Military, so it just seemed like a natural extension of all my fantasies. In my naiveté, I was gonna be John Wayne, and kick some Commie Butts. Who was it that said "What fools these

243

mortals be?" You are soon to learn just how much that statement applied to me.

I need to give you just a bit more background about my teenage life outside of my career as a performer. This has a direct bearing on my future brief career in the military.

During WWII, (and in the years following) there sprang up around the country a bunch of organizations with semi-military activities. The most popular ones had little kids dressed up in sailor suits, practiced marching, knot tying, and things like that. These organizations had names like "The Sea Cadets", or "The Maritime Brigade". (I don't know if those organizations exist anymore.)

But wearing a sailor suit, and marching with a bunch of little kids did not hold any appeal to me. However, these organizations came up with a way to attract older boys, and hang on to the ones already in the organization who were outgrowing the "kid stuff". They formed a unit called "The Marine Division" of the Maritime Brigade. Kids had to be 14 or older, and got to wear real US Marine Corps uniforms, formed drill teams with real guns, taught marksmanship, went on maneuvers, and all that macho stuff. They held regular weekly meetings every Friday night at a local Armory.

When I found out about it, I was hooked. I joined in a heart-beat at age 15, and quickly rose in the ranks. I became a crack shot, won lots of medals in competition, and was leader of our rifle drill team. We entered and won close-order drill competitions, served as honorary firing squads at military funerals, and even marched in all the big parades down New York's Fifth Ave. The "biggies" were the Thanksgiving Day Parade, St. Patrick's Day Parade, and other local area events. I gotta tell ya. I was in "Hog Heaven". Although

I was too young to serve in WWII, I was living vicariously playing at being a Marine. I think I outgrew that activity only when I became old enough to do it for real. Check this out.

That's me, leading our detachment in some local parade. Note the Guide-on I'm carrying. That spot in the line of march carried over into my Air Force days. I think I was about 16 at the time. Those activities in my teens prepared me for my actual military service later on. In my free time, I lived a whole different lifestyle that one would expect of a kid in show business. And I made some great friends among the older boys in the outfit. That's some of them in the pic below. And that handsome dude (second from the right) is "macho man". Ha!

Under the circumstances, I'd have to say I was thankful that I had a reasonably normal life in my later teens. I was fortunate to have a full time job (Saturdays only) that permitted me to have some fun with the rest of my buddies. I think that by that time in my life, I really didn't care if I continued my acting career. Actually, I was leaning towards the military. I liked being a "leader". Ah! The light dawns. That's why I became a TV director.

O.K, That brief side trip down memory lane sets the stage for what happened next to "Jughead".

When the military beckoned during the Korean war, someone set me up with an interview with an Air Force Colonel. Ostensibly, to chart a course that would get me into Aerial Gunnery school once I enlisted.

My dreams (misguided ones) came crashing down. He told me that it would be highly unlikely that I'd get to choose that assignment. In addition, the Air Force didn't need aerial gunners anymore. The new Bombers all had the guns aimed electronically, and human Gunners, as such, were obsolete. *"Besides, he said, why throw your career away with a four year enlistment. This Korean thing is probably going to blow over in a few months, and you won't see any action"*. He continued on. *"Look. Why don't you fulfill your military obligation by joining a reserve or Air National Guard unit. That will exempt you from the draft, you'll be in the Air Force Reserve, and you can have the best of both worlds. You can continue with your radio career, and serve your Country at the same time"*. With that, he gave me the name of someone to contact at an Air National Guard unit in Westchester County N.Y., (45 minutes north of where I lived), and suggested I go see them.

Now, who am I to argue with a full bird Colonel. He seemed to know what he was talking about, and I appreciated getting his advice. After all, the Korean Police Action was going to be over in a few months, (in his judgement) so my enthusiasm for becoming a "warrior" was dampened big time.

That Air Force Colonel was only right about one thing. By joining that Air National Guard Unit, I was able to keep playing "Jughead" for one more year. But his estimate of a quick end to the Korean hostilities was way off the mark. In fairness to him, I don't think anyone expected Communist China to get involved.

There is a funny side to my military career which I might as

247

well come clean about. But it was a trifle embarrassing at first. Actually, I was so pissed off, I couldn't believe it was happening to "macho man".

When I signed up to join that Air National Guard unit, the First Sergeant (who was filling out my enlistment papers) was extremely friendly, and seemed genuinely pleased that I'd be joining the outfit. He was very impressed with my show business background, and thought it would be neat to put me in the "Special Services" slot. But he had a big problem. He had just filled that slot the prior week with another enlistee, and he had only one other opening available at Group Headquarters. And that was the "Chaplain's Assistant" slot. (Don't you dare laugh!)

He explained that it would be no problem whatsoever. He'd just put my name on the roster (in that Chaplain's assistant slot), but I'd be free to do all sorts of things with my time. I could plan entertainment events for the outfit, organize recreational activities, etc.

He then asked, "*Uh? By the way, what religion are you?*" When I replied Catholic, he said "*Great, so's the Chaplain. But he's a great guy, and he doesn't need any help. Besides, the only time he 'says' Mass, is when we have a once a month weekend drill. We have so many Italian Catholics in the outfit, they all fight over who will be his alter boy... you won't have to do anything.*"

Yeah ! Right! But as it turned out, he was right. At least for the first few months. I organized the outfit's annual dinner dance, and arranged some very special entertainment following dinner. I got Bob Hastings to come up and sing for the troops. I even organized and trained a marching drill team. Remember now, we were what they called "Weekend Warriors". We only had to show up every Friday night for training, and one weekend a month. Consequently, I was still free to play "Jughead" on Saturday mornings. So, you're asking, what about the full weekend drill each month that you had to attend? Let's just say I showed up late. The First Sergeant liked the job I was doing for the outfit the rest of the time, so he covered for me until I reported in around mid-day Saturday.

Let me quickly inject what kind of an Air National Guard unit I had joined. I was assigned to a HQ detachment that supervised about six Squadrons responsible for setting up (and operating) long range RADAR installations. Each squadron was capable of independent operation. Our job in HQ was primarily administrative. In theory, the individual squadrons function was to set up in advance positions to detect the approach of enemy aircraft. While the squadrons trained, I had a cushy job.

But then, all hell broke loose. The real hell was happening in Korea, when the Chinese got involved. My "hell" began when we were notified that our Air National Guard unit was being called up into full time active duty, We were told to get our civilian affairs in order, and that we were becoming Regular Air Force personnel.

Heck, that wasn't the bad part. I was eager to go. I had a fantasy to fulfill. The bad part happened when the First Sergeant called me into his office and told me he had bad news for me. Now that we were to become Regular Air Force, he didn't have the freedom to just let me continue my Special Services job. Unfortunately, he said, I was in the Chaplain's Assistant slot, and the Chaplain wanted to know where the hell his assistant was!

I was crushed. Me, the self styled "Warrior" ending up as a

Chaplain's Assistant. I'm being called to active duty, and going to war, as a glorified clerk and alter boy to a non-combatant Priest? How was that possible? I considered going AWOL. It would have been better getting shot as a deserter than living through that disgrace. ☺

But I thank my lucky stars, it all turned out fine in the end. However, the beginning was a trifle dicey.

I had my orders, so I dutifully reported to the Chaplin's office on the 2nd floor of headquarters, and knocked on his door. A deep voice bellowed *"Come in"*. I entered with all the military bearing I could muster, snapped to attention, and crisply saluted, saying. *"Airman Stone reporting, SIR!"*

This big guy, with the insignia of major on his uniform jacket, leaned forward, placed his hands on the desk, and with a slight smile said. *"Let's see, you were assigned to me about three months ago, right? I was wondering when the hell you were finally going to show up. At ease…and take a seat"*.

That was my introduction to one of the greatest guys I ever met in my life. But the remainder of the conversation that day set me back a bit, and went something like this.

Major: You're Catholic, Right?

Me: Yes Sir!

Major: Were you ever an Altar Boy?

Me: No Sir!

Major: I hear you are an actor, Right?

Me: Yes Sir!

Major: Good! I hear that actors are good at memorizing
        things. Right?

Me: Yes Sir!

Major: Good!... Memorize this!

And with that, he reaches into his desk drawer and pulls out a
big laminated card, and tossed it across his desk in my direction. It
had a lot of stuff written on it in Latin. I was looking at a" script",
in a language totally foreign to me. It was the lines the altar boy
has to say in response to the things the Priest says during Mass,
and it even gave cues, for when to ring the dang bells.

Major: (With a wry smile on his face) OK Airman Stone.
         Nice meeting you. You've got two weeks to learn it.
         Dismissed.

That was my introduction to Father (Major) Charles Gordon.
A big bruiser in stature, a "Regular Guy", great sense of humor,
and a decorated veteran of the 2nd World War, (having seen action
with an Army Mountain Division in Europe). He could also play
piano with the best of them. (Whore House Honky Tonk style.) He
was beloved by every man in the outfit.

Even though I memorized all the mumbo jumbo on the card
he gave me, I never had to be an altar boy. I could have sold tickets
to all the guys who had prior experience and were eager to do it.

251

Fortunately, Major Gordon understood and sympathized with my unhappiness at being a Chaplain's Assistant, and even though we got along just great, he told me he had no problems with my changing job descriptions if I could work it out.

I may not have been born rich or good looking, but I sure was born lucky. (My Mother would say "It was my Guardian Angel watching over me".)

Remember the guy who was put in the Special Services slot one week before I enlisted? Well, he came to me one day, and confessed he didn't know what he was doing in that job. He told me I was far more qualified to do it than he was, and did I want to switch if we could get approval. DUH?

We pulled a few strings, and everybody was happy. AND GUESS WHAT? He was a Protestant. But I soon discovered the real reason why he wanted to change places with me. The Officer he had worked for, and my new boss, was a total *)%^&*%! Oh well! War is hell!

Now, lets see how I can tie all this nonsense into my radio acting career .

A soon as we were activated in the Regular Air Force, our outfit was sent to an Air Base in New Hampshire (about a 5 hr. drive North of NYC), for intensive training, getting equipped with new Radar gear, and boxing everything up in preparation for shipping out to our overseas destination.

During that period, I was able to get weekend passes (hey, I worked in HQ), and would make the long drive home on Friday nights so I could still do the program on Saturday mornings. All in all, from the time I joined the Air National Guard, until we shipped out, I guess I was able to do the show for almost another year.

See! My early teenage "Marine Division" training came in handy. I still carried the "Guide-On" flag. Only this time, marching at the head of real "Warriors". ☺ I think this was our final "Pass-in-Review" parade before shipping overseas.

My unit's overseas destination was St. Johns, Newfoundland (Don't laugh). It was out of the United States, a "foreign" country (Canada), so we were qualified to draw "overseas pay".

When we reached our destination, our unit grew much bigger, and we became a "Division HQ" with all sorts of new job assign-ments. I became the NCO in charge of Ground Safety. I figured that change in assignment, I'd be making a bigger contribution to the war effort. All of our squadrons were then dispatched to desolate locations throughout the far north, (Labrador, Thule, and assorted Ice flows). Their function was to set up their Radar equipment in a "DEW Line", (Defense-Early Warning) across those Northern wastes. It seems our country was deeply concerned that Russian bombers might try to attack us while we were getting our butts kicked in Korea, and these distant radar sites would give advance warning if Russian planes took the obvious direct Polar route to get at us.

I was responsible for investigating and reporting any and all accidents in our Division, and formulating safety procedures. I did a lot of traveling to those God forsaken and bitterly cold sites. But the highpoint in my Military career (back at Headquarters), was being appointed "Gun Captain" in charge of a 50 Cal. Anti-Aircraft machine gun in case any attack did come. I got that assignment because I was the best shot in the Division. (See! All those years "playing" soldier were not wasted.).

Now, if any of my kids or grandchildren ever ask, *"What did you do in the Korean War?"*, I don't have to "gulp", and sheepishly reply… *"I was a Chaplain's Assistant"*.

One final note about that. When I briefly served as a clerk for our Chaplain, Major Gordan, I happened to be going through his files one day looking for something he needed. I came across a document from his earlier days in World War II. It was a certificate that awarded him the Bronze Star for "Gallantry in Action". It seems he picked up a rifle and captured 9 Germans during the Battle of The Bulge. I couldn't believe my eyes. A Chaplain taking up arms? When I asked him about it, he simply replied, *"Heck, it was either them or me, and it wasn't going to be me"*. He would have been awarded the Silver Star, but because he was a Chaplain, the Army brass didn't think they should make too big a deal about it. I say again, he had the respect of every man in our outfit, and no one respected him more than I did. I knew a real "Hero".

I thoroughly enjoyed my duties as Ground Safety NCO. So much so, I was seriously thinking of re-enlisting when my 2 years were up. But many of my friends told me I had to be nuts to give up all those years of experience in Show Biz. Besides, I discovered that it was better being an Officer than an enlisted man. I gave it some hard thought, and finally decided I'd go for the discharge, get a college education under the G.I. Bill, and set my sights on a career as a TV director. Actually, while stationed in Newfoundland, I still kept my hand in at entertaining, and would help out the Base Special Services guys by acting as M.C. for special events.

Check out the sexy mustache on the guy holding the mike.

Now, back to Show Business. While I was out of the United States, I know of at least two guys who replaced me as "Jughead". Billy Lipton played the part briefly. Then Arnold Stang was hired .

By then, Arnold was on his way to becoming quite popular as a TV personality. I think he was even doing "his thing" on the Milton Berle TV Show, playing "Francis" the stagehand around the same time he was doing "Jughead". (Arnold had worked with Berle on his earlier radio show.) Another of the memorable characters Arnold played was the voice of "Top Cat",  which was an animated spoof of the popular and zany "Sgt. Bilko" TV series. Arnold went on to do a ton of work in TV and Motion Pictures. I couldn't even begin to list them all here.One of my favorites was his role in "It's a Mad, Mad ,Mad, Mad, World".

Ironically, when I was researching his incredible list of credits on the internet, I came across this quote.

'Arnold got his start in Old Time Radio as "Jughead" on the "Archie Andrews" Show, replacing Hal Stone who was in the Army during the Korean war.'

Well, that bit of trivia was wrong on two counts. Humph! Me, in the Army? No way! And Arnold got his start in Old Time Radio long before he played "Jughead'. As a matter of fact, he was around as long as I can remember, and often played other characters on our show long before he took over for me as "Jughead".

I can prove it. Check out the cast list of the "Theatre Guild Program" on page 265 in the next "scene". (I'll wait.) ☺

Years later, as a director, I used my friend Arnold in some TV commercials. As a matter of fact, one of them was even "Banned in Boston". The concept was to have Arnold standing next to a very buxum, leggy, chorus girl as his foil. She was wearing "short shorts", which were the fad back then. The staid Boston viewers complained to the sponsor, saying it was too sexy. Actually, the viewers were probably paying more attention to her than the commercial spiel that Arnold was delivering.

To finish up with this part of the book, I'll just say that when I returned from the service, I got the part of "Jughead" back.

Rosemary Rice told me that the NBC sales people assembled the cast, and told them they were again trying to find a sponsor for the show, and they felt that Arnold's celebrity status just might help with a sale. But because of my long service on the show, NBC was torn in making the decision about having me play the role again. In democratic fashion, they left it up to a cast vote.

I don't think Arnold minded relinquishing the role back to me. He was much too busy in TV, and making a lot more money than he could have earned doing a non-sponsored Kid's radio program. Besides, he probably saw the handwriting on the wall, and realized radio was fast becoming extinct because of TV.

It goes without saying. I was gratified to hear that my old friends wanted me back. But I think Hastings just wanted me around so he'd have somebody to pick on again. How do you like that? And me, a returning "war hero". ☺

Act 3

Scene 3

(Music) "Fly Me to the Moon...Let Me Play Among the Stars"

(Establish music, then fade under)

(CUE NARRATION)

Appropriate theme music if I do say so myself. I not only played among the "stars", but worked with them on any number of occasions. And not just on the "Archie Andrews" show.

Throughout my radio career, I had the good fortune to perform on many other programs, but certainly not in any major or starring roles. But it did give me the opportunity to get to know some really talented people. And throughout this book, I've attempted to show how their successful early careers in radio led to even greater success in TV and films.

In the next few pages, I'll take you on a quick trip down memory lane and introduce you to some of these folks. You old-timers in the audience (especially those in the OTR hobby) will undoubtedly recognize these names. And those of you familiar with TV and films of the 60's, 70's, and 80's, may recognize the faces. If not from that period, you may have seen them in re-runs.

259

MASON ADAMS: Mason Adams had an incredible career in Radio. "Pepper Young's Family" was one of his better known shows. From 1947 to 1999, he went on to do many TV shows and films, . Do you youngsters remember him on "Lou Grant"? And recently, on "West Wing".

LEON JANNEY : Leon played many roles on radio. Another busy actor. He did some films as a young boy in the late 20's. Following his radio career, he did lots of TV, ("Edge of Night", "Another world", Etc.) I also worked with Leon many years later when he was a TV spokesman for a local NY brewery.

ARNOLD MOSS: One of the deepest and most melodious voices in the industry. His later career was spectacular. "Star Trek", "Alfred Hitchcock", "Bonanza" to name a few. And roles in about 20 major films, like "Viva Zapata", "Bengal Brigade" etc. He made a great swarthy villain.

ROBERT DRYDEN: Despite his youth, his specialty on radio was playing very old men. He worked on the TV series "Naked City", which was shot in N.Y. in the late 50's, and "The Edge of Night" soap. Bob appeared in a number of films in the late 70's. A very versatile actor.

260

ANN THOMAS: This lovely and fun lady was a joy to work with. Following her radio days, she did a few notable TV roles, among them "Suspense" and "Chevrolet Tele-Theatre". In film, she did "Duffy's Tavern" (as "Miss Duffy"), "Midnight Cowboy", and about 5 others.

BETTY GARDE: After Radio, Betty did a lot of TV. "Suspense", "The Honey-mooners", "Mr. Lucky", "Twilight Zone", "Ben Casey", "The Real McCoys", various soaps, and to name a few films; "All the Way Home", "Cry of the City", "Caged", "Call Northside 777", and "The Prince Who Was a Thief".

OLIVE DEARING: Another fine actress. She played on many of the early live TV dramas, appearing often on "Philco Playhouse", "Kraft Television Theatre", "Suspense", "Ben Casey", "Perry Mason", etc. Her film roles; "Caged", "Ten Commandments", and about 8 others.

JOSHUA SHELLY: Now we go from charming to chuckles. Josh was a very funny guy to be around, but a serious actor. He made over 30 TV appearances, and about 10 films. He was absolutely great in "City Across the River", master-fully playing the part of "Crazy Perrin" .

JOSEPH JULIAN: Joe was another popular NY radio actor who made the "visual" transition. He did stints on early TV soaps "Edge of Night", "As the World Turns", and in dramatic series', "Perry Mason", "The Untouchables", "Hawaiian Eye", "Alfred Hitchcock Presents", etc.

JOE DE SANTIS: A super nice guy and one heck of an actor. He was very active in radio in the 30's/40's. He scored big as a "heavy" in menacing roles in Motion Pictures. "Slattery's Hurricane", "I Want to Live", "Al Capone", "The George Raft Story", "Beau Geste", "The Professionals", and numerous TV shows as well.

KARL SWENSON: Another fine gentleman. Karl ended up amassing an incredible amount of credits. Over 115 TV appearances, and over 30 films. He did lots of westerns and action films. "Son's of Katie Elder", "Ulzana's Raid", "North to Alaska", "Major Dundee", etc.

RALPH CAMARGO: Try as I might, I couldn't trace Ralph's career after Radio. But I just had to include him on the list of really nice people to work with. He was warm, personable, and very talented. He had a ready smile, and a kind word for everybody. One of the "good guys".

WARREN STEVENS: When I first met Warren, he had just returned from WWII, having served as a pilot in the Air Force. While working in radio, he was also doing plays in summer stock , and studying at the Actors Studio. His big break came on Broadway in the hit play "Detective Story". From that point on, his career skyrocketed. In the 50 year period between his first movie appearance, Warren performed in over 3 dozen films, and literally hundreds of TV shows. I had to place this mini bio of Warren at the end of this section. There's no way I could do justice in just a few sentences. He performed on practically every top TV series at one time or another. "Cannon", "Happy Days", "The Odd Couple", "Gunsmoke", "Hawaii Five-O", "Mission Impossible", "Lassie", "The Virginian", Cimmarron Strip", "Bonanza", "The Rat Patrol", "Big Valley", "Dr. Kildare", "Perry Mason", "The Andy Griffith Show", "Ben Casey", "Have Gun Will Travel", "The Untouch-ables", "Alfred Hitchcock Presents", "Bat Masterson", "Leave it to Beaver", etc. etc. etc. (phew!)

Anyway, you get the idea. Many radio actors I worked with had a long life after TV came along. And it was those actors who had theatre training, in addition to their radio experiences, who became standouts in the new visual medium.

Speaking of the "Theatre", one of the more interesting radio shows I worked on was "Theatre Guild of The Air". (How's that for a segue into a new topic?) "Theatre Guild" was considered to be one of the more prestigious radio dramas of it's day. And the atmosphere connected with it was almost like the "Opening Night" of a Broadway play. Complete with Theatre Programs.

UNITED STATES STEEL

Presents

The
THEATRE
GUILD

On The
AIR

"DEAD END"

Program for February 24, 1946

Sunday Evenings Over WJZ and Stations of the

AMERICAN BROADCASTING COMPANY

UNITED STATES STEEL CORPORATION

welcomes you to

THE THEATRE GUILD ON THE AIR

production of

"DEAD END"

by SIDNEY KINGSLEY

starring

Richard Conte ♪ Alan Baxter

Joan Tetzel

with

Anne Burr   Ann Thomas
Agnes Young   Danny Leone

Director	*Producer*	*Musical Director*	*Radio Adapter*
HOMER FICKETT	GEORGE KONDOLF	HAROLD LEVEY	PAUL PETERS

ARMINA MARSHALL, *Executive Director*

General Supervision by THERESA HELBURN *and* LAWRENCE LANGNER

CAST

(In Order of Their Appearance)

Speaker	Henry Sharp	Hunk	Maurice Gosfield
Gimpty	Richard Conte	Mrs. Martin	Agnes Young
Angel	Michael Artist	Francy	Ann Thomas
Tommy	Danny Leone	Drina	Joan Tetzel
Spit	Harlan Stone	Kay Mitchell	Anne Burr
T.B.	Arnold Stang	Jack Hilton	John Flynn
Freddie	Ronald Liss	Mr. Griswald	Dwight Weist
Philip	Alastair Kyle	Policeman	Henry Sharp
Doorman	Jay Velie	First G-Man	John Flynn
Baby-Face Martin	Alan Baxter	Second G-Man	Dwight Weist

Introducing the Play and Players, LAWRENCE LANGNER

GEORGE HICKS, *reporting for U. S. Steel.*   *Announcer,* NORMAN BROKENSHIRE

"The Theatre Guild on the Air" was performed in a converted Broadway theatre. Converted, in so far as soundproofing the large stage area was concerned, wiring the place for microphones, and the construction of one of the most unique "Control Rooms" I've ever seen. The Director was Homer Fickett , a burly, balding, heavy set guy, who made his "directing" a part of the performance.

They constructed a totally glass enclosed booth right in the middle of the Orchestra pit. (It looked like the "Pope-mobile" without wheels.) It was about 8 feet long, and maybe 6 feet deep. Homer stood inside during the performance, so the audience could see him (from the back) as he made like an orchestra conductor.

He didn't share the spotlight. The Engineer sat at his console much lower in the booth. Homer Fickett was the only one visible. I recall he wore a white suit. (It might even have been a tuxedo.)

And it was dress up night for the performers also. I guess you could call it semiformal. The men (and in this particular show), the young boys as well, all dressed in dark suits, shirt and tie. The females in the cast wore demure and dark colored cocktail dresses.

When the audience arrived, the front stage curtain was down. They were handed programs as they were being seated. A few minutes before show time, the curtain was raised, and Lawrence Langer entered to polite applause. He then introduced the show to be performed that evening, followed by introductions of the cast, (one by one), based on their star status or size of their role in the production. (We had been waiting off in the wings for that moment). Then Homer Fickett was introduced. I recall he made an entrance along the front row orchestra section, took a bow, entered his glass encased capsule, the lights dimmed, and Homer threw the cue for the Overture. As you might imagine... the marriage of radio drama, sophisticated theatre atmosphere, and the showmanship of our director, Homer Ficket, made for a most unusual and memorable radio production. The studio audience loved all the trappings. That production of "Dead End" included many of the people that I mentioned throughout the pages of this book. It was a "Who's Who" of young actors who were in the business back then.

Before I get back to more of the "Misadventures" of our days playing on Archie Andrews, I might as well mention some of the other shows I did after leaving my teens.

I did a bit on the "Ethel Merman Show". Talk about Show Business legends! Wow! She certainly had a unique style and delivery, but she seemed warm and good natured, despite her "brassy" exterior. I think I played an NBC Page. But I didn't have to wear the uniform. Radio didn't take things to that extreme.

I also did a bit on the "Slapsie Maxie Rosenbloom Show". What a character. The only photo of Max that I could find was from around the time that he was the Light Heavyweight Boxing Champ. (1934) When I worked with him, he was probably around 50. Slapsie Maxie Rosenbloom was enamored of Show Business, but his acting talent

267

primarily consisted of playing "muscle heads" or "punch drunk fighters". (Hmm? I wonder how much acting was required to pull that role off?) Slapsie Maxie Rosenbloom fought about 300 times in 16 years. (1923-39) His record? 208 wins-39 losses-26 draws.

Maxie definitely was a celebrity of sorts. He began making movies in 1933, while he was Champion of his division. He also owned a popular night club in Hollywood for years. It was a watering hole for movie celebrities, so Max, through their influence, started making even more films. Would you believe 63 all told? Many times playing "himself" in them. That's why NBC decided to capitalize on his celebrity status, and built a comedy show around him. I don't think it lasted too long, It might even have been a brief summer replacement one year.

Another program I was hired to do was "The Henry Morgan Show", but I don't remember the first thing about it. Henry started as a local NY radio disk jockey. He had a very wry and irreverent style of humor and became quite popular. So much so, that NBC created a half hour network comedy show for him. Henry Morgan went on to do quite a bit of television, particularly as comic relief on the early TV "Panel" shows.

During my late teens & early 20's, I also started performing on some of the live TV dramatic shows such as "Robert Montgomery Presents". In reality, Mr. Montgomery didn't have much involvement with the actual production, and just showed up to do the programs opening introduction. It was simply a way for NBC to capitalize on his status as a well known motion picture star, which contributed immensely to that program's popularity. He might also have been involved in story selection for the show. I didn't have much contact with him on the set, but he seemed very affable, and I enjoyed meeting him.

Another popular live TV dramatic series I appeared in was "The Kraft Television Theatre". (Very similar in story content and approach as the "Montgomery" program). The one thing that stands out in my mind about that experience was meeting someone who was making their first professional acting debut and who went on to have a wonderful career. A super nice guy whose name was Fred Gwynne. He and I were in a few scenes together (just small parts), playing a couple of young soldiers. If his name doesn't immediately conjure up an image in your mind, how about his starring roles in the TV comedy sitcoms, "Car 54, Where Are You?", and as the monster "Herman Munster". Fred eventually broke away from that comedy mold, and went on to do some classic dramatic work in films and TV.

Since I was also a fan of many of the Old Time Radio shows, it was a treat for me to work with the stars of some of my favorite programs. For example, "Superman" aka Bud Collier, and Ray Johnson, Paul McGrath of "Inner Sanctum" fame.

Then too, having to be around the halls of NBC so often, one couldn't help but bump into some famous actors who were working there on any given day. One in particular comes to mind. The motion picture star Pat O'Brien. (It seems that the nicer the person was, the easier it is for me to remember the event.) But on the other hand, I suppose the opposite is also true. But I'm pleased to report that the vast majority of them were quite affable, as well as approachable. Pat O'Brien's "Irish charm" was incredible.

I probably spent about 15 minutes chatting with him, sitting on one of the benches outside the 3rd floor studios. We were both studying our scripts (for two different programs) and he struck up the conversation. Once he found out I was part Irish, I was his new best friend.

Referring back to the opening theme music for this chapter in my life, ("Fly Me to the Moon, Let Me Play Among the Stars"), I would have to say that the "brightest star" in the "Entertainment Firmament" that I had contact with was the legendary Al Jolson.

Mr. Jolson had an incredible career in the early days of Vaudeville, and very first talking picture. He was undeniably the top singer/entertainer of his day. Fortunately, his singing career and unique vocal style had a tremendous resurgence of popularity following the 1946 release of a movie about his life, "The Jolson Story", starring Larry Parks. That prompted NBC to star Mr. Jolson in his own very popular radio program in the late 40's.

Once again, an older Al Jolson captivated a whole new younger audience. And am I ever glad he did. I was mesmerized by his inimitable style, and the classic songs he performed. I took advantage of my access to all the NBC studios, and sat in on his rehearsals whenever possible, and went to many on-air performances of his show. They were broadcast from studio 8H. That show needed the largest radio studio in the world to fill all the ticket requests. (NBC eventually ripped out the raised stage (and huge seating area) to convert 8H into a spacious TV studio that was needed to accommodate the scenery for live TV shows). For Jolson's broadcast, I always had front row seats, sitting among many of the old time show business greats that Jolson attracted. He was an intense flamboyant showman. Just look at that face opposite. He had a devilish gleam in his eye, and an impish grin. I thoroughly enjoyed watching that man work. His energy was palpable. I even got to chat with him briefly on a few occasions during breaks in his rehearsals. Those were the days!

I'm somewhat inhibited and reluctant to get back to talking about my career in the shadow of such greatness. But if I don't, the book would end here. So...where were we? Oh yeah! Talking about some of the extremely talented performers I worked with over the years.

As regular cast members of the "Archie Andrews" show, we were indeed fortunate to work with many radio actors who eventually achieved stardom in television. That's not to say they weren't already big names in radio, but their recognition by the masses was only possible when they became other than a voice, and their faces became instantly recognizable.

On any given Saturday, our show's director might need to book an actor to play a variety of roles. In the supporting cast, the script might call for a shopkeeper, a tradesman (of some sort), a cop on the beat, an auto mechanic, a lady in distress, etc.

These characters would be written into the script to create situations that "Archie" and his friends might encounter, and help develop the comedy story line. It usually resulted in our teenage characters getting in, then out, of all sorts of trouble.

We were blessed with an incredible talent pool in New York. I'll just mention a few performers that we always enjoyed working with, and who ultimately achieved great things in TV and the movies.

One of my all time favorites was Art Carney. Whenever we needed a cop, or fireman, or construction worker, he was probably the director's first choice. He had, as the world was soon to discover, a great sense of comedic timing and could do many character parts. I loved it when he was hired to play "Jughead's" zany "Uncle Herman". What fun! And I seriously doubt I have to mention the fame he was later to achieve.

Then too, we would also use (whenever possible), a very fine dramatic actor named Ed Begley. Ed was an institution in Old Time Radio. Extremely talented, and a master at the difficult and "heavy" dramatic roles. He also carved out a niche for himself in TV and Motion pictures.

Of course, the younger generation is certainly familiar with the accomplishments of his Son, Ed Jr. For what it's worth, I had a numerous contacts with other members of the family. Ed Begley Sr. had a brother Martin, who was a fixture around the halls of NBC. A charming guy, he seemed to be very involved in getting performers to donate their talents to appear on one of the Catholic

religious programs of the time. It might have been called "The Avé Maria" hour. I recall Martin got me involved a few times. (Of course, that made my Mother very proud.) I guess she considered that by donating my acting services to the church, it might help absolve me of the many sins that her son was bound to commit.

But years later, I was to have an even closer relationship with another member of the Begley family. Martin's son, Martin Begley Jr., had spurned the acting profession and went into the technical side of TV. In my fledgling days of directing, he was my audio engineer on many productions.

There also was an event that happened during one of the early episodes of the "Archie" program that involved Ed Begley in a very frightening and dramatic way. I suspect the world will hear about it for the first time in these pages.

As the cast was assembling for a rehearsal of the following weeks episode, Vinton Hayworth drew young Charlie Mullen and me off to one side, and wanted to give us a bit of friendly advice. He said one of the other actors who was going to be in the show that week (and had not shown up yet) was an actor named Danny Occo. Vinton told us that Danny had a terrible reputation, and an unbelievable mean streak . He warned us not to clown around with the guy (in our normal exuberant teenage fashion), because this Occo fellow could get very nasty.

Right about that time, this huge guy walks into the studio, and gruffly acknowledges the rest of the cast (but didn't crack a smile.) When he was introduced to Charlie and me, he just grunted and looked away disdainfully. We were beginning to understand Vinton Hayworth's advice and warning about this guy.

Danny Occo was not only huge, towering over us teenagers, but his overall appearance was intimidating. He had a Prussian crew cut, a very swarthy complexion and a dark bushy mustache. He looked like one of those evil Turkish prison guards in the movies.

The script called for "Archie and Jughead" to be in a scene with some "big troublemaker", played by Danny Occo. (As I mentioned previously, the directors often cast people who physically resembled the part for the benefit of the studio audience.) So just as we were standing at the mikes, ready to rehearse the scene with this evil looking individual, the studio door opened, and in walks Ed Begley with a big grin on his face, saying something like *"Hi everybody, hope I'm not interrupting. I just have to give Vin Hayworth a quick message."*

He hardly got those words out of his mouth, when Occo, who was standing next to us up on stage, screams out; *"What the hell are you doing here? I told you I never wanted to be in the same room with you, you bastard!*

Ed defiantly yelled back, *"Go to hell, you big son of a bitch!"*

With that, Occo leaps off the stage and bellows at Begley, *"You #%^*μf , I'm gonna throw you the hell out of here"*. As he got near Begley, he shoved him. From Charlie's and my vantage point up on the stage, it then looked as if Ed Begley spit right in Occo's face. With a deafening roar, Occo lunged for him, Begley ducked, then ran like hell up the steps of the audience section, with Occo following close behind. We were all stunned. Ed begley escaped out the upper exit doors, and Occo, his face livid with rage, came back down the steps, back up onto the stage, and approached the mike where we were both still standing in shock. (And trembling in abject fear, I might add.) He glared at the two of us and said. *"What the hell are you two looking at?"*. Before we could timidly respond, the whole cast erupted in gales of laughter.

We had fallen victim to a huge practical joke.

At that point, Ed Begley came back into the studio through the doors at stage level, grinning from ear to ear. Danny Occo, upon seeing how perplexed and frightened we were, put and arm around our shoulders and wanted our forgiveness, claiming he was put up to it by the others. That great actor Ed Begley, assisted by his good buddy, Danny Occo, put on the performance of their lives.

We vowed to get even some day with Vinton Hayworth who masterminded the whole thing. We did have our revenge down the road (probably more than once), but I don't remember the circumstances exactly. But you can be sure it never came close to the classic joke that those three played on Charlie and me.

It turned out that Danny Occo was one of the sweetest guys around. He was as kind and gentle as he was big and mean looking. Danny was another actor that I hired when I became a director later on, and we'd often talk about that fun event.

 Another really friendly and warmhearted individual was the actor Ross Martin. I always enjoyed working with him when he played a supporting role every so often on "Archie". Ross also lived out on Long Island, so when we'd finish a performance, he'd wait around until I concluded signing autographs for some of the audience members, and we'd ride home on the subway together. He was great company.

I was thrilled for his later success in Hollywood and enjoyed his portrayal of "Artemus Gordon", (Bob Conrad's sidekick), on the hit TV series "Wild, Wild, West". But that was only one of many credits for this very popular actor. He did about 35 films and appeared in over 90 TV episodes, starting in 1950 and on up until his untimely death (heart attack) in 1981. He did many of the very popular TV shows during his exceptional career; "Fantasy Island". "The Love Boat", "Mork & Mindy", "Hawaii Five-O", "Charlie's Angels", "Barnaby Jones", "Sanford and Son", "Ironside", "Laugh In", "Wonder Woman", Wagon Train" and a host of others.

I bumped into him many years later, (the late 60's) and had a treat in store for me. I was in LA directing some commercials and was having dinner with some ad agency people at "Mateo's", a trendy LA restaurant . There was a stir in the room, and who should walk by my table but Lucille Ball, accompanied by none other than my old buddy Ross Martin. He looked briefly at me for an instant as he was passing, stopped, turned and looked again, and a big grin spread across his face. I jumped up, we hugged, while a bemused Lucy looked on. Ross introduced me to that show business icon and briefly explained to Lucy about our past radio days together. We mentioned something about *"needing to get together one of these days"*, and they continued on to their table. But our schedules never permitted it. It turns out Ross was busy directing Lucille Ball's TV series "Here's Lucy", and I had to get back to New York. I would have enjoyed "talking shop" with him and reminiscing about the good old days. But the great "new days" for each of us were definitely more financially rewarding.

Another fun event was when the great character actress Hope Emerson was booked to appear on the "Archie" program in the early years. Hope was a huge woman, probably about 6'5", and was very broad shouldered. And her performance on our show was as a last minute replacement for the woman who was originally cast in the part.

Our program writer Carl Jampel would often get his story ideas from current events. The Circus was in town, so he decided to write a script about Archie and Jughead getting involved with Circus performers. He worked out a deal with the circus PR people, and we were to get the actual Fat Lady from the circus side show to play the part. For some reason or other, she chickened out, and our director frantically set out to book the biggest actress he could find in New York. (Remember, I told you we often cast for the benefit of the live studio audience.) Hope Emerson won the part hands down.

The script called for "Archie and Jughead" to be in conversation with the circus Fat Lady, and at some point, she has a line about "Jughead" being cute, and picks him up to give him a crushing hug. Little did I expect that for the actual broadcast, Hope picked me totally off the ground as if I were a bag of groceries.

I was shocked, but I didn't lose my place in the script. I knew my lines by heart. All "Jughead" had to do was keep screaming…

"Put me down! Put me down! Put me down!"

The audience was hysterical. I guess there was something to be said for casting people who looked the part. But I certainly didn't anticipate actually doing the physical sight gag . But we often indulged in those kind of antics on that show.

Hope Emerson belied her size and stern demeanor. She was a gentle giant, with a big heart.(Obviously.) She carved a niche for herself playing rough and tumble Westerners, and whenever a big woman was needed for effect, Hope would be considered for the part. Of the 30 or so films she made, her big role, in my opinion, was as the evil, cruel, and menacing female prison matron in the motion picture "Caged".

Ooops! I just realized something. I got sidetracked talking about some of the famous people I encountered over the years of working in radio, and I have yet to mention the many announcers that we used on the Archie program. Some of the names might be quite familiar to you folks. I could be wrong, but I think this was the order of appearance over the years.

1) Ken Banghart: Did many NY originated programs.
2) Bob Shepard: Eventually went to LA and worked on TV game shows.
3) Tex Antoine: Also famous as a NY Weatherman, and a cartoonist of note who created the character "Uncle Weatherby" used in his weather casts.
4) Bob Sherry: Did the show for many years, particularly during the "Swifts" sponsorship.
5) Dick Dudly: Our last announcer who also worked on the show for many years.

Every one of them, without exception, had great voices, often worked on many other shows, and were a delight to be associated with. Sorry I don't have photographs of them to share with you.

OK, moving on to another topic. As a lead in, let me brief you on another live TV appearance I did in the late 40's. It was on "The Lanny Ross" show. But I wasn't playing a part. I was simply being myself. In those early days of TV, radio programs and TV shows were peacefully coexisting. In some cases, NBC used exposure on one medium to promote the other. In this instance, Lanny Ross, who had been a popular singer many years earlier, was given a shot to host a daily live TV variety and interview show in the afternoons. Since NBC was still trying to promote (and possibly sell) "The Archie Andrews" radio show, I was invited to be a guest on Lanny's show one day to be interviewed about my career, and also talk about what it was like to play "Jughead". Gee! I was a celebrity guest star. Aw Shucks!

Obviously, I didn't succeed in helping us find a sponsor, but you can't blame a guy for trying. Which brings me to the next topic. Over the many years the "Archie" show was on the air, the NBC Network's Sales, Publicity and Promotion departments did what they could to sell and promote the program.

And obviously (again), the Sales Department also fell short of their goals. Of the nine years the show was on the air, we were only sponsored for short durations. (Swifts Meat products for a year, Kraft Foods for 13 weeks). But one possible explanation was the fact that NBC's major sales efforts went into selling prime time programs. That's where the bigger audience ratings were. Those night-time shows carried bigger price tags, which meant they earned bigger bucks for the network.

Undoubtedly, the NBC's Promotion and Publicity departments probably helped us become the top rated Saturday daytime radio show for much of the program's existence. (However, I'd like to think the cast had a little something to do with it.) Nonetheless, the NBC publicity department kept us busy with numerous photo shoots.

These pictures are not in any particular order or time frame. Heck, I barely remember having had them taken. But these sessions were never a drag. We had fun, because we all got along so well together. We even considered them social events of sorts, outside the businesslike atmosphere of the broadcast studio. I had to restore many of these photos from old faded copies, so I apologize for the quality. But at least you get the idea, right?

Keep in mind that our primary listening audience were kids ranging in age from 6 to around 15/16, so we had to appear as "goofy" teenagers. Well, maybe we were "Type Cast" after all.

Rosemary (Betty) and Gloria (Veronica) became very close friends over their years together on the show, socially as well.

Do you think it bugged Jughead that Archie always got the girl? Does that look like envy on my face? Naw! More like boredom! It probably bugged Archie more...because Jughead was always hanging around! ☺

During the year of the Swift Sponsorship, we did quite a bit to promote the program's relationship with that particular client.

If you look closely, Mrs. Andrews, (Alice Yourman) seems to be offering Mr. Andrews (Arthur Kohl), Archie & Jughead some Swifts Premium Franks to eat. How can I tell? Because they're still wrapped in the cellophane label! The "Boy's" are supposed to be busy repairing an NBC microphone. Hey! I just showed up for these photo sessions. Don't blame me for the ideas.

Another product/show tie in was the "Souvenir Program" that was handed out to the studio audience. (See following page.)

The cover of it (folded) gave the product pitch. The inside was used by the kids to get autographs after the broadcast. Sorry, you'll have to turn the book sideways to see. But you can probably use the exercise after sitting and reading for so long.

286

They sure put us to work with this promotion. Following the broadcast, they would bring out and set up two long tables at the front of the stage. The 6 principal cast members would sit in a row, and sign their names on these things, as the kids filed past.

Did we get paid extra for this additional time we put in each week? I don't recall, but I seriously doubt it.

Hey! I just found another photo from the "microphone repair session". The plate containing the Swifts Franks is now sitting on the table in front of Archie.

Another form of promotion and publicity was to be mentioned in NBC's Publicity department's weekly press release. The one on the following page features a dumb article about me. These were printed on fairly large sheets, so I reduced it to fit on the page. You won't be able to read the text too well. But I fixed that problem.

The date of this issue is March 22, 1946. But since this book is about me. I'll save your eyesight and blow up that section.

Jughead the Showoff Fails as Fish-Flipper

NEW YORK, Mar. 00 — Harlan Stone, Jr., who plays the well-meaning but bungling Jughead in NBC's "Archie Andrews," (Saturdays, 10:30 a.m.), occasionally finds that real life imitates fiction a little too closely and is too much like an "Archie" script.

Harlan is a second class Boy Scout working for his art merit badge and training to be a patrol leader. He takes his Scouting seriously, and his over-anxiety got him into a typical Jughead situation on a recent Scout outing.

The boys had been fishing and, after much effort, caught just enough for a meager meal. Harlan

Harlan Stone, Jr.

was permitted to fry the fish on the beach. Showing off a little, he tried out the fancy flip-flop technique of restaurant window pancake artists. Result—all the fish slid out of the pan and onto the sandy beach.

Harlan tried his best to wash off the sand but somehow the fish persisted in remaining gritty. So the troop lunched on marshmallows.

There! That better?

The stories were sort of trite, but what the heck. There wasn't too much of interest they could say about a teenager, right?

Besides, they had to crank out these press releases every week, so one can't get too creative with that sort of deadline.

My friends at Archie Comics Publications recently sent me a copy of an ad that was hanging right outside the door of ACP Chairman, Michael Silberkleit's office. (See following page.)

I'm not sure where or how or it was used, but I have a sneaking suspicion that it may have been a full page ad in an "Archie Comics" issue.

Maybe even the back cover?

Remind me to complain to ACP. The actors didn't get any name credits in it. Better yet, I should have fired my agent....except radio actors didn't use agents back then.

If I'm not mistaken, the photo below was taken at a cast party held in the "Rainbow Room" atop the RCA building. I believe we were celebrating the one year sponsorship of the "Archie" show by the Swifts Meat Packing Company. What? No hot dog stuck in the cake instead of a candle? (They certainly missed a good PR opportunity).

But it seems our celebration was short lived. Swift cancelled the sponsorship shortly after. (Do you suppose someone at the ad agency got ticked off because the Rainbow Room didn't serve Swifts Premium Franks at the luncheon?)

Left to right: Alice Yourman, me, Bob Hastings, Gloria Mann, Arthur Kohl and Rosemary Rice.

This photo was also taken at that same celebration.

The tall gentleman is Carl Jampel, the writer for all of our "Archie" episodes. (That's nine years worth of weekly scripts.) The two gentlemen on the right are most likely Client and NBC brass. That is of course, Archie and Jughead flanking Carl Jampel.

One other promotion and publicity "biggie" that was done for the program, was a big photo-story spread that appeared in one of the Motion Picture/ Show Biz entertainment magazines of the late 40's.

The only way I could show you how they laid it out, I had to have the 1st page printed sideways. Oh well, it's exercise time again.

ARCHIE ANDREWS

An exclusive MSP Radio Parade picture script . . .

Bob Hastings as.................Archie Andrews
Arthur Kohl as..................Mr. Andrews
Gloria Mann as..................Veronica
Perry Como as..................Perry Como
Harlan Stone Jr. as.............Jughead
Rosemary Rice as................Betty
Alice Yourman as...............Mrs. Andrews

When Archie Andrews ambled into the den to ask his Dad for an advance on next week's allowance, how was he to know he'd run smack into the annual battle of the income tax blank? Instead of the extra buck he'd been hoping for, all Archie got was a lecture on economy and orders to go sit down and think it over. Gosh, how could a fellow ever get ahead in the world without the funds for a flashy wardrobe, or the dough for dreamy dates? His parents didn't seem to realize inflation had set in.

Then suddenly as he lay there on the couch, Archie's eyes felt so heavy he had to close them, and bong, he was a millionaire. First thing the new Archie did was call up his pal Jughead, give him the good word, and hire him as a personal yes-man. 'Course Jughead rushed right over to the Andrews' house (only now it was a movie-style mansion with six swimming pools and a soda fountain in every room).

293

First off Archie bought the local theater for his private use. He and his girl Veronica could drop in anytime and have the manager run off fourteen cowboy movies in a row. And since he'd become such a man of money, Archie'd hired the chief of police as a bodyguard and acquired his own shoeshine boy.

Archie's Mom had been after him for a long time to take some singing lessons so just to keep her happy he started looking for a voice coach. "They tell me this fellow Como is quite a singer," Jughead suggested. "Well then, he's the man for me," Archie declared and in no time flat there the two of them were sharing a mike, with Perry giving Archie tips on how to do right by a tune. Nothing was too good for Archie now.

Archie was easily the most popular guy in town—the girls fought for a chance to sit at his feet, friends he hadn't seen for years turned up to shake his hand, and even Dad couldn't do enough for him. Archie had put Dad on an allowance but he kept coming around for more— always looking for an extra hundred thousand or so. No wonder Archie had to lecture him on extravagance.

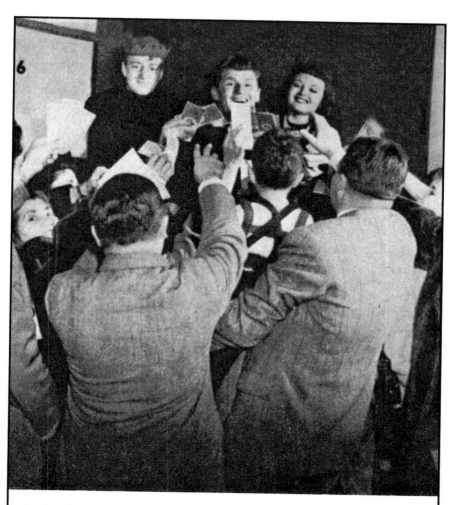

As for Mom, when he found a speck of dust on the first mink coat he bought her, Archie tossed it out and gave her another. Everywhere he went he was the center of attraction. Then one morning he got to thinking—maybe he was popular only because of his money. This life of luxury was getting him down. He must put a stop to it. He took all the cash he had and began to hand it out to strangers on the street.

When he came back to his office he was a poor but happy man, without a worry in the world. That is he was until Betty, his secretary told him some men from the Treasury Department were waiting for him. It seems they'd come to collect his income tax and he didn't have a single cent to give them. And as if that weren't bad enough, Jughead called to warn him that

Archie Andrews may be heard every Saturday morning at 10:30 EST over the NBC network.

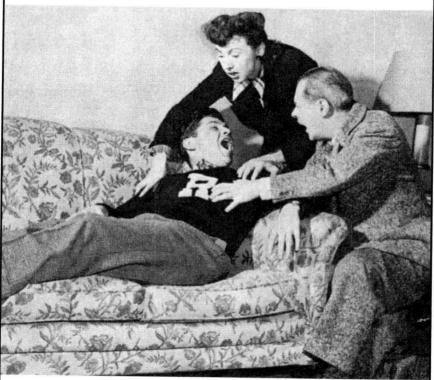

the local police accused him of causing a riot by giving away all his money and they too were hot on his trail. It was the darkest day of Archie's entire life. Then just as he was being marched off to jail, he felt a hand on his shoulder and heard his father's voice. "Wake up, son, I want you to take my tax blank down to the postoffice." Archie sat up with a start. "Gee, Dad," he yawned, "it's great to be poor again."

As you might imagine, we all had a lot of fun back in those good old days. The "Archie" cast was a tight knit group, and everyone thoroughly enjoyed our long association. We got along great. But that's true of the many wonderful performers mentioned in these pages.

Obviously, we all had personal lives outside of our career, but would find time to socialize when our schedules permitted. I recall going to parties hosted by Alice Yourman and Arthur Kohl at their residences. I recall I even had to practically carry a very inebriated Sound Effects man home one evening following a party at Alice's. We would also have annual cookouts and picnics at Ken McGregor's sprawling property overlooking the Hudson River.

The photo below is from a cast party my family and I hosted at our small Country Club. That's Bob and me horsing around with our last director, the wonderful and fun loving Ken McGregor.

As I mentioned earlier, It was great fun working with some of my fellow cast members after I became a director. Like the time I used Bob Hastings in some "Tastycake" TV spots. See next page.

Obviously, one of the best photos ever taken of Mr. Hastings during that shoot. It shows his best side. (Love ya, Bobby)

THE TALE ENDS-DIM THE LIGHTS- CUE THE CURTAIN

Curtain Calls

Ah Yes! Curtain Calls. The aphrodisiac of all theatrical performers. To hear the waves (or ripples) of applause as one takes their bows following a performance can be heady stuff.

Even the performers in Radio who worked in front of a studio audience had applause ringing in their ears. And would you believe?... We still do.

But before getting to that, I have two things to share with you of an educational nature. (I want to improve your mind at no extra charge.) Do you know why, when the actors take their bows following a stage performance, they are referred to as "curtain calls"? (Do you even care to know?) O.K., I'll tell you anyway. ☺

In the theatre, the stage is a lot wider than what the audience sees. (But you knew that.) That area is called the "wings". Close to the stage was an area for the "switchboard" or lighting panel. It controlled all the lighting effects on the stage at any particular time during the performance. Today, modern lighting switchboards are a fraction of the size seen here (circa 1940).

In modern and refurbished theatres, the lighting control panels are miniaturized and computerized and placed at the rear of the audience area. One also now finds the audio controls panel there since stage performers often wear mikes nowadays. (What ever happened to actors who could "project" their voice so that they could be heard in the upper balcony's?) Anyway......

Off to one side, along the wall of the backstage area, was the "rigging". A system of ropes and pulleys that controlled the raising, lowering (or opening) of the stage curtains, as well as long grid pipes for hanging lights. Even scenery, hung from pipes, could be lowered or raised. They were called "backdrops" or plain "drops".

Because, (are you ready?) Ta! Da! They were "dropped" into position by these guys on the ropes. (Snare drum-rim shot!) As you well might imagine, accidents happened if the stagehands failed to "drop" things slowly. I mention all this to explain why so many ropes were needed along that side wall. OK? Now you will better understand the explanation about the term "curtain calls".

All of these stagehands, the electrician guy, the rope pullers, the prop men, took their cues from the Stage Manager, (who was positioned immediately off to the side of the stage out of view of the audience). He stood at a tall podium, on which rested the entire script of the play, with all sorts of notations marked on it. That was his "cue" sheet so he could let all the stagehands know when to do something during the performance.

When the curtain was lowered after the final act, and the audience (hopefully) began applauding loudly, the performers would gather on stage quickly, ready to take their bows. But, to be heard over the noise of the applause, the stage manager would call out loudly to alert the performers *"Curtain going up"*, (so they wouldn't be seen picking their nose perhaps), then call to the stagehands, *"Curtain up"*. Then, to again alert the performers, call out *"Curtain coming down"* (to make sure they backed up and not get bopped on the noggin). That sequence was repeated time and again as long as the audience kept applauding. Hence the term "Curtain Calls". How 'bout them apples?

Incidentally, the stagehands in the photos used to illustrate this bit of trivia actually worked on "Life With Father" at the Blackstone theatre in Chicago over 60 years ago. Wow! Memories!

A fun thing that often happens at the end of each performance, (in theatres world wide), is that the cast often counts the number of curtain calls that they take. If it was an appreciative audience, you might hear, *"Wow! We had 12 curtain calls tonight"*. Or, *"Gee, what a dead audience, we only had 5 curtain calls tonight"*.

One of the most incredible displays of almost unlimited curtain calls I ever witnessed, happened back in 1949 . But I wasn't a member of the cast. I just happened to be in the audience that night.

Ray Bolger, the famous comedic song and dance man, was appearing in a hit Broadway musical comedy titled "Where's Charlie". (If his name doesn't ring a bell with you "youngsters", he played the "Scarecrow" in the mega-hit film "The Wizard of Oz".) But in 1949, Ray had just won the prestigious "Tony" award as "Leading Actor-Male" for his show stopping performance in "Where's Charlie". His BIG number was singing and dancing to the hit song from that musical, "Once in Love With Amy".

When the curtain fell after the last act, the cast began taking their curtain calls to a standing ovation. When it was Ray's turn, (the Stars of the show usually came out last for their bows), he was met with thunderous applause. He stood there bowing for the longest time. The pit orchestra then started playing "Once in love With Amy", and Ray Bolger reprised the number. And reprised the number, and reprised the number. The audience wouldn't let him off the stage. They kept applauding, and he kept doing it (goofing around, talking to the audience, doing variations, etc). It was only after the hands of the audience became too sore to clap any longer that he said his final "Goodnight", and skipped off the stage. I didn't think to time the event, but I bet the audience got another half hour's worth of entertainment during his "curtain calls". Actually, the curtain didn't keep going up and down. It would have worn out the poor stagehands pulling on those ropes. What a thrilling experience it must have been for Bolger. It certainly was for the audience that evening. And more than likely, for the audience every night of that hit musical's two year run on Broadway.

Now, you may well ask, what has all this got to do with a

book about the Golden Age of radio broadcasting? Well, radio actors often took "curtain calls" or bows in front of a studio audience following a performance. (Where is it written that one needs a curtain to do that?)

But that's not the point I wanted to make. Radio performers from those good old days <u>are still taking</u> bows and "curtain calls" to this very day. And that's all due to the OTR hobby (Old Time Radio) that many people share; (the collecting, trading, and discussion about many of the popular radio programs of those bygone days).

These folks are die hard enthusiasts, often fanatic, about this hobby. They have kept alive the art form of radio broadcasting to an incredible extent. They hold many annual conventions in many of the major cities throughout the country. And we, (the actors from that by-gone era), are invited to attend these conventions as honored guests. I gotta tell ya! It's a thrill to be remembered and appreciated for the body of work we did so long ago.

I know I speak for all the old time radio performers when I say we truly appreciate the thousands of fans in the OTR Hobby for making us feel that the performances we did back then (as well as now, at conventions) still give them many hours of listening pleasure. Thanks, all you fans out there.

These OTR "Conventions" are usually held over a 3 day weekend. We actors do recreations of the old programs that we once performed on, and get to meet and greet many of our old fans. (As well as the younger ones, who are familiar with the roles we played because they collect recordings of those old broadcasts.) Some fans also join in and play supporting roles in the recreations.

Below is a photograph from one of those OTR conventions. In this instance, it was the one held by FOTR (Friends of Old Time Radio), an annual event in the NY-NJ area .This photo is from their 1994 Convention, when they invited as many of the original cast members of "The Archie Andrews" show that they could find.

Back row, L to R. Joan Shay (Mrs. Andrews), Bob Hastings (Archie), Pat Hosley (Veronica), Dick Dudley (our last announcer), Rosemary Rice (Betty) and Ray Erlenborn (sound effects guru). Front row: Yours truly (Jughead), John Rayburn (Mr. Andrews).

Pat Hosley worked on the "Archie" show often, and when Jane Webb (our last "Veronica") couldn't attend the convention, Pat subbed for Jane beautifully. John Rayburn is a fixture at these conventions, has a great announcing voice, and stepped in to play the father for us.

But the surviving "Archie" cast members don't always play

the parts that we are closely identified with. Bob Hastings and Rosemary Rice are often asked to recreate episodes of "Ethel & Albert" (and other shows). At a recent OTR Convention in Cincinnati, I also played "Oogie" in a recreation of "A date With Judy".

A few years ago in Los Angeles, at a SPERDVAC convention (The Society to Preserve and Encourage Radio Drama, Variety and Comedy), many Radio oldtimers assembled to do a number of recreations. One was written by the famous Radio writer and director, Norman Corwin, who was there to direct us in his original radio play, "My Client Curley". The photo below is of that cast.

Left to right (the one's that are visible), Gil Stratton, Jr., Art Gilmore, Cliff Norton, (Tommy Cook, Alice Backes in the rear), then Janet Waldo, and me, (playing a few small parts in that epic).

Gil Stratton did a lot of west coast radio; "My Little Margie", "Lux Radio Theatre", "Yours Truly, Johnny Dollar", "This is your FBI", etc. Gil was later to become a famous sportscaster.

Art Gilmore had an illustrious career in Radio as an announcer on "Amos n' Andy", "Dr. Christian", "Stars over Hollywood", "The Adventures of Red Ryder", etc., and also as an actor in a number of radio dramas. In TV, Art played on "Emergency", "Adam-12", "The Mary Tyler Moore Show", "The Waltons", etc.

Cliff Norton was a very busy actor in Chicago in early radio. "Terry and the Pirates" was just one of his shows. He went on to do a lot of work in TV, and has a great gift for comedy.

Tommy Cook is best remembered for playing Little Beaver on "The Adventures of Red Ryder" and Junior on "The Life of Riley", along with roles on "Blondie", "Lights Out", etc.

Alice Backes, in addition to doing quite a bit of radio, such as "Lux Radio Theatre", "Barrie Craig, Confidential Investigator", etc., was also quite active in television.

Janet Waldo amassed many credits. She played the title role on "Meet Corliss Archer" for 12 years. Also, appearances on "The Adventures of Ozzie and Harriet", "One Man's Family", and as the voice of Judy Jetson in the TV cartoon series, "The Jetsons".

Another popular OTR Convention is the one held each year in Seattle, hosted by REPS (Radio Enthusiasts of Puget Sound). The organizers came up with a nice concept this year. For a very modest donation, any OTR fan could pose, seated in a chair, and have their picture taken with a bunch of us radio performers as background (see opposite page). L to R: Gil Stratton, Art Gilmore, Esther Geddes, Tyler McVey, Sam Edwards, and some other bozo.

That's Fred Korb in the hot seat. Fred is an incredible OTR fan, and came all the way from Chicago to attend the Seattle Convention. He graciously consented to let me use his photo for

RADIO - THEATRE OF THE MIND
REPS SHOWCASE X

this book. I selected Fred as my OTR Fan "Poster Boy" because he's fairly typical of the many hundreds of really nice people who attend these functions. Without their intense interest and support of the Hobby, the shows from the "Golden Age of Radio" would be just a far distant memory. And we, the performers, would have no reason, (or a stage), upon which to keep taking our "curtain calls".

You might be interested to learn that the gifted Professional Photographer who took those pictures at the Seattle Convention was none other than Christopher Conrad, the son of the late (and well known actor), William Conrad. Bill Conrad was best known for his portrayal of Marshall Matt Dillon on the radio series "Gunsmoke". You older TV fans will remember him in the starring role of "The Fatman" series and many, many other shows.

In addition to these OTR clubs scattered throughout the country, there are now many web sites and chat rooms devoted to the hobby. Lois Culver hosts a fun chat room on the internet every Thursday evening. (Lois is the widow of actor Howard Culver, star of the radio show "Straight Arrow".) There are also numerous dealers who sell copies of all the popular shows on cassettes and CD's. There is even an OTR Digest published daily on the internet. The administrator (moderator, Web Master, or whatever you call him) is the same #μ)≤∂ßᵃæ who talked me into writing this book. I won't mention any names, but his initials are Charlie Summers, aka "Curly Top". (I have as much fun zinging him as I do Bob Hastings.) It's called "get even time".

Another group who also deserve a curtain call; my friends at Archie Comics Publications, John Goldwater and Louis Silberkliet (the original publisher's of the Comic Book.) Without them, the "Archie" program would never have existed. They are deceased now, but their two sons carry on the tradition. In the photograph opposite, that's Michael Silberkleit standing at left, (the current Chairman of ACP) behind his father Louis. John Goldwater is standing next to the "Archie" cutout, with his son Richard (far right), now President of Archie Comics Publications.

2 Families Keep Archie in Step With Era

The New York Times / Joyce Dopkeen

(Photo curtesy of Archie Comics Publications)

Well I guess that about wraps things up. I said what I had to say, and probably more than I should have in some instances. The only thing I feel the least bit guilty about is picking on my good buddy Bob Hastings. That last picture of him that I shared with you (from the rear) really didn't do him justice. So to make amends, I'm now including a front view. We'll bring him back for another "Curtain Call". I'm feeling generous.

That's him! Honest! You can tell by the eyes. ☺

Oops! I almost forgot. I promised to give you folks some suggested reading in case you're new to the OTR Hobby, and wish to learn more about it. The books I now mention are just the few I have read, and some others that are considered to be excellent reference material for many of the old radio programs.

Most authors usually do a formal bibliography. I'd just as soon keep it conversational. I'll also include some of those web sites I mentioned earlier, (in case you are into computers and the internet) and want to learn more about OTR that way.

A very entertaining book was written by a friend of mine, Dick Beals. (You can read the title opposite.) Dick and I never worked together in the early years, because Dick began his career in Detroit, playing youngsters on some very popular programs like "The Lone Ranger" and "Challenge of the Yukon". He eventually moved to LA, where he worked on many shows, also doing character voice's for animated cartoons. But his biggest claim to fame (and fortune) was as the voice of" Speedy Alka-Seltzer" for those TV commercials. Dick and I finally met at an East Coast OTR Convention some years back, and since then, we've had many opportunities to work together as performers. A fun guy!

Another book that I enjoyed reading was Arthur Anderson's "Let's Pretend-A History of Radio's Best Loved Children's Show", published by McFarland & Company. (Do you suppose the reason I enjoyed reading it is that I'm mentioned in it?) Not really. It's an in depth look at the radio program that I told you about earlier. I only mentioned the kids from that show that I worked with. There are many more that Arthur talks about. I understand the book is currently out of print. I was able to get a copy out of my local library. But Arthur has a few copies left that he sells at the NY-NJ FOTR Convention.

Speaking of that big annual convention. The principal force behind that organization is Jay Hickerson. Jay has written a 560 page reference work, listing over 6,000 network, regional, local and syndicated radio programs. (Giving broadcast dates, sponsors, etc,) and often includes a brief description of the show with the names of one or two cast members. For further information, contact the author Jay Hickerson @ Box 4321 Hamden, CT 06541, or Fax (203) 281-1322 - E-mail: JayHick@aol.com

Another book that many people consider to be the "bible" of OTR Radio Programs is one that was published in 1998 by the Oxford University Press. The title, "On the Air; the Encyclopedia of Old Time Radio", written by John Dunning. I found a copy in the reference section of our library. It lists everything. Facts, dates, cast members, descriptions of the shows, and a super great index so you can look up all sorts of things. I have only one bone to pick with the author. He does not have a very high opinion of the "Archie Andrews Program". I think he used the term "Frantic" or something akin to that word in the description. (Obviously, he never heard the show as a young kid.) It was never designed to appeal to adults. Oh well! Win some, lose some. ☺

Another book about old time radio was published in a very

unique style. Each page consists of some great "illustrations", (drawings of the performers, and or characters they portrayed) and some text describing the history of the program, and cast members. Here's a sample page. Can you guess why I selected this one?

That book's title, and names of the authors, are readily visible. Frank Bresse, responsible for the text, was a radio actor of note in the LA area, with the very popular "One Man's Family" among his many credits. Bobb Lynes is a wonderful artist who also happens to be a huge fan of Old Time Radio. Both are neat guys, and are very involved in SPERDVAC, (the LA areas annual OTR Convention.) To learn more about the book, contact Bobb Lynes.. P.O. Box 561, South Pasadena, CA 91031 or E-mail @ iairotr@hotmail.com

I know that a great many other books have been written on the subject of OTR, and many are very recent publications. A large number of them have been researched and written about specific programs. A very nice young man named Martin Grams has written quite a few, but I'm not able to comment on them because I haven't read them.

I confess, I am not a collector of material about Old Time radio. I think I'm considered to be one of the "collectibles". I only know about the programs that I personally worked on. It always amazes me to discover the amount of current interest in the subject by the folks in the hobby, and many of them recall more than I do about the character I played.

As I mentioned earlier, in addition to tons of books about OTR, there is an ongoing flood of material that you can access on the internet. And to find out more about the TV and film careers of the folks I mentioned, a great site is www.imdb.com. As for sites specializing in radio topics, just plug your search engine into the subject "Old Time Radio" and a whole bunch of sites are available.

One that I am most familiar with is >oldradio.net< . That's a daily "OTR digest" with content of interest to a great many Old

Time Radio fans who post questions (and answers) about any and all matters connected with radio shows and the performers who appeared on them. It's very informative, and often fun. (The membership is free, but donations to help support it are welcome.) Subscribers get copies of the Digest via E-mail, and I frequently encounter questions by the fans. My response is then posted in the next day's issue. I might even initiate a comment or two if I can shed any light on a particular topic. (See... I even get to take "Curtain Calls" on the "electronic" stage.)

Another form of ongoing activity is the infamous OTR Chat Room on the internet, hosted by the always charming and fun loving Lois Culver as moderator, room monitor and zoo keeper. I can't promise that the topic always concerns Old Time radio. There's a lot of kidding around, (among friends), and it's a three ring circus trying to keep up with all the various threads of conversation between the participants. And everyone who signs on, as long as they are nice people, are enthusiastically welcomed to join in the "party". If you're on the Net, you can find out how to get there by contacting Lois at >lois@acoder.net<

Well, I don't know about you, but I'm exhausted. It took a long time and energy to put this book together, and I can't believe I've reached the end.

I hope you enjoyed your guided tour down memory lane, and my recollections about "The Golden Age Of Radio".

But just in case you didn't. Please turn page.

Aw! Relax Folks.... Relaxxx!

What did you expect from a "Jughead"?

BYGONE DAYS PRESS
ORDER AND SHIPPING FORM
"Aw...Relax, Archie! Re-Laxx!"

DATE _____

NAME _____

ADDRESS _____

CITY_____STATE_____ZIP_____

PHONE_____FAX_____E-MAIL_____

Number of copies_____Unit Cost: $26.00 = _____

Shipping:*   _____

Tax**   _____
(Az Residents only)

TOTAL: _____

CHECK #_____CREDIT CARD#_____

_____ EXP DATE:_____
cardholder signature

* Shipping and handling charge: $4.00 per book. $2.00 per additional book to same address.

** Arizona Residents please add 6.3% sales tax on cost of book(s) only.

Mail order form and payment to: BYGONE DAYS PRESS
P.O. Box 4418, Sedona, AZ, 86340

Toll free number to order by phone: 1-866-237-5664 or Fax at 928-282-3858

To order directly on the Internet: Go to www.by-gone-days.com